the beginning of knowledge

The fear of the LORD is
the beginning of knowledge;
fools despise wisdom
and instruction.

PROVERBS 1:7

THE BEGINNING OF KNOWLEDGE - Christ as Truth in Apologetics
2nd Edition

Published by:
R3VOLUTION PRESS
Chapel Hill, TN

Jacket and interior designs by Scott Alan Buss

All Bible verses, unless otherwise noted, are taken from the *English Standard Version* (Copyright © 2001 and used by permission of Crossway Bibles, a division of Good News Publishers).

R3VOLUTION PRESS Books are available at special discounts for bulk purchases. R3VOLUTION PRESS also publishes books in electronic formats. For more information, please visit www.R3VOLUTIONPRESS.com or www.FireBreathingChristians.com.

ISBN 13 Digit: 978-0-9838122-8-9

Printed in the United States of America

For my Lord, the Personal Source of all truth, life, beauty, and love.

The fear of the LORD is

the beginning of knowledge

contents

The fear of the LORD is

the beginning of knowledge

contents

Pride, Grace, and Stupid Little Kindergartners

...in your hearts honor Christ the Lord as holy, always being prepared to make a defense to anyone who asks you for a reason for the hope that is in you; yet do it with gentleness and respect...

1 PETER 3:15

Those poor, stupid little kindergartners.

There they were, all around me, just as they had been the day before. But they were different to me now. Very different. Whereas yesterday I was one of them, now they mostly just kind of...well...*bothered* me.

On that day there was something a more than a bit troubling about them. Something sad. Something frustrating. Something *wrong*.

Part of me saw them as sympathetic, another part as just pathetic.

Such was the emotion and attitude that had washed over me in the moments after I had...get this [drumroll, please]...learned to tie my shoes *all by myself.*

1

Please allow me to repeat:

All.

By.

Myself.

For my entire life prior to that transformative event, I'd been one of the ignorant masses. But on that fateful day I became one of the enlightened elite. I learned an important truth and I applied that truth. As a result, I found my way to the other side – out of the darkness and into the light.

I was truly *special* now (just like Mom always said I was).

From this new position of enlightened specialness, I couldn't help but feel for those poor saps I'd left behind in The Land of The Unenlightened.

How could anyone *not* pity those poor paste-eating fools? I mean, they couldn't even tie their own shoes!

I certainly didn't speak of these truths aloud on that day. I even smiled and played nice with my inferiors. But I was thinking it. And I was feeling it. Just as had happened many times before and has happened many times since…and not just inside of me, but inside of you as well.

That's what knowledge does to us. Every time. Apart from Christ and His Gospel, we are doomed to remain in that self-centered, self-serving, hypocritically arrogant and destructive rut. This rut is so warm and so comfortable to naturally self-absorbed mankind that we will not only ride it to the bottom, but, unless God intervenes, we will do so while imaging ourselves to be something quite bright, good, and worthy of adoration.

With this truth of human nature – *our* nature – in mind, we are well served to take a moment to shine the perfect light of the Gospel onto *ourselves*. Only that light can purge self-centeredness from our systems and prevent us from sharing in the shaky foundations of self-absorbed, four-year-old shoelace masters. Only that light can prepare the way for biblical, Christ-centered apologetics, and so it is there – to *Him* – that we must first go and always strive to remain.

a·pol·o·get·ics [*uh*-pol-*uh*-**jet**-iks]
noun
the branch of theology concerned with the defense and
rational justification of Christianity.

The aim of this book is to equip believers with an introduction to Christ-centered apologetics that is not only approachable to all believers, but **downright exhilarating**. New believers and mature Christians alike oughta be flat-out *jazzed*. Each of us should be thrilled at the prospect of learning more about the living, loving Lord who is the "beginning of all knowledge and wisdom" and has purposefully called *us* to proclaim that beautiful truth throughout His creation. This is not another collection of cornbally sentimental appeals to self-centered emotion or yet another series of man-centered philosophical strategies and tactics for winning debates or better articulating the "evidence for God". It is instead a call to *biblically* gear-up, man-up (woman-up, too), and take it to the enemy, with "it" being the supernatural Gospel of Jesus Christ accompanied by the undeniable, unstoppable, Christ-centered defense of the faith "once for all delivered to the saints" (Jude 1:3) against which *every* enemy stronghold must fall and even "the gates of Hell cannot stand" (Matthew 16:17-19).

It is in this spirit that *The Beginning of Knowledge – Christ as Truth in Apologetics* has also been crafted to address a particular concern. The recent trend in the professing Christian subculture towards apologetic works and worldviews that are built more and more upon man-centered philosophy and psychology at the inevitable expense of Christ-centered biblical theology must be tackled head on and without apology, so to speak. This weed must be uprooted so that the garden can flourish.

The hope of this book is that, Lord willing and by His grace, it might be used to move His people *away from themselves* and *towards Him* as the perfect, sufficient source of *everything*, including their apologetics. *The Beginning of Knowledge* is not to be confused with *The Exhaustive, Complete Presentation of Knowledge*, a book that has not actually been written and a mission that has certainly not been undertaken here. This work *is* offered as a relatively simple number that points to Him boldly and clearly in a spirit of grace as He defines and provides it.

The primary mission and objective of this work is to emphasize that *every* area of the Christian life – certainly including our apologetics – is only as good as it is explicitly focused and built upon the *Person* of Jesus Christ *as revealed in His perfect Word*. Every step taken away from His nature as the basis for understanding *anything* in favor of man's standards for understanding the same – from Christ-centeredness to man-centeredness – can only lead towards darkness. This is a most challenging and beautiful truth that *every* Christian must not only grasp, but adore and *apply*. They can do so by the grace of the very Person who lives within them, giving them eyes to see, ears to hear, and a heart's desire to understand more and more and *more* about the object of their supernaturally inspired affection. How cool is that?! (Hint: *Very*.)

So it is the hope that herein the reader will find a bridge away from self and towards Christ as the source of all knowledge.

For a more detailed examination of the Christ-centered apologetic presented here (often described elsewhere as *presuppositional* apologetics or *covenantal* apologetics), the reader is encouraged to seek out and enjoy the excellent works of Dr. Greg Bahnsen (*Always Ready, Presuppositional Apologetics, Pushing the Antithesis*), Dr. K. Scott Oliphint (*Covenantal Apologetics*), and Cornelius Van Til (*Christian Apologetics, The Defense of the Faith*).

Readers are also strongly encouraged to check out *How to Answer the Fool – A Presuppositional Defense of the Faith*, an excellent video presentation of biblical apologetics in action. Sye TenBruggencate's fearless, passionate, and loving defense of the Person of Christ is an inspiration that will benefit believers seeking a better understanding of Christian apologetics, as well as encouragement that *each and every one of us can defend the faith in power and confidence*, by God's grace and for His glory. While not all are called to globe-spanning, large-scale ministry, **all believers are called to be apologists at some level**.

Though apologetics has long been understood as a branch of theology, in recent history, particularly in the West, Christian apologetics have been shifted from a God-centered, theological foundation onto any number of man-centered, philosophical counterfeits. Lord willing, that is going to change…one biblically grounded, Christ-centered apologist at a time.

CHRIST-CENTERED APOLOGETICS

"I am the way, and **the truth**, and the life. No one comes to the Father except through me."

JESUS, IN JOHN 14:6
(BOLD EMPHASIS ADDED)

Our intense inclination toward self-centeredness is hardly an affliction confined to our kiddie years. In a very real sense, and particularly in modern western culture, it is our ongoing embrace of self-referential standards that has enabled us to drag a "kiddie year mentality" right on into and through adulthood, middle age, and even our later years. The Fall in Eden echoes strongly in this. Our embrace of self over God – and self-centeredness in place of God-centeredness – has led us into a pronounced and accelerating downward spiral, and, apart from the supernatural intervention of God, we will ride that death wave until it finally crushes us against the rocks of His truth.

Our personal rejection of God is centered on a rejection of His person as revealed in His Word, which provides us with the theology and doctrine that define who He is. Christian doctrine and theology are revelations of His person. They form the basis of a Christian worldview, but they are not to be treated as or imagined to be merely sets of facts or rules by which one ought to govern their lives. They are much, much more than that; they are details concerning who He is. They are revelations of His nature, His personality, and His identity.

The world rejects these things because it hates Him *personally*. The personal aspect of theology and doctrine cannot be overstated.

When God the Spirit through the Apostle John says, "If you love me you will keep my commandments," we are being taught with clarity something that is counterintuitive to all self-referential, worldly minds. Self-centered inclinations encourage the *separation* of God's nature from His law and any other uncomfortable revelation of His nature as contained in His Word. Yet, the challenging clarity of Scripture remains, unwavering and without qualification: "*If* you love me you *will* keep my commandments."

When we view the depths of theology and doctrine as anything less than *intimately* related to the *person* of Christ, we find it easy to dismiss them as unnecessary. Once deemed unnecessary, our dismissal of biblical theology and doctrine at any point of conviction enables us to substitute the Christ of the Bible with a counterfeit Christ we craft in our head using self-serving emotions, traditions, and desires as our guides.

However, when we understand that it is the very *person* of Christ – His desires, likes, dislikes, and very nature – that is contained in His Law and in every other jot and tittle of His Word, then we will, by His grace, desire to uncover, learn, and embrace every minute detail. Every microscopic morsel and perceived triviality will then become the object of our intense, awe-stricken curiosity and passionate pursuit.

When we find ourselves attracted to a person, we want to know more about them. We want to know what they like, what they don't like, what they think, and why they think it. The more intense our interest in a person, the more intense our interest in their *personality*.

The husband-wife relationship is the pinnacle of such expression in this life. It is hardly coincidental that the marriage relationship is described in Scripture as the magnificent, mysterious reflection of the relationship between Christ and His Bride, the Church (Ephesians 5:22-32). In this, we are presented with a beautiful illustration of and model for the adoring pursuit and application of knowledge where the nature of an adored *other* is concerned.

For the unbeliever, Christ is the ultimate Other whom they have rejected in favor of *self*. Their love is *self*-directed, their standards are *self*-referential, and their worldview is relentlessly and irrationally *self*-justifying, regardless of the logical, ethical, or moral impossibility of it all.

Such love of self is hatred of God. They hate Him *personally*. Were they able to kill Him, they would certainly do so (see: the crucifixion).

Their animosity is *personal*, and this personal hatred from the world extends to all who are in Him (Mark 13:13; John 15:18).

As such, both the object of Christian apologetic defenses and the environmental context in which such apologetics are practiced must both be understood to be *personal*.

FIRST FOR THE LOVE OF GOD
(AND THEN FOR LOVE OF THE LOST)

For I am not ashamed of the gospel, for it is the power of God for salvation to everyone who believes, to the Jew first and also to the Greek. For in it the righteousness of God is revealed from faith for faith, as it is written, "The righteous shall live by faith."

ROMANS 1:16-17

Apologetics is personal.

We are not defending a set of rules.

We are not defending a set of principles or probabilities.

We are defending a person; *the* Person of persons, our Lord Jesus Christ, the Word made flesh.

As our faith is defined by the Word of God, and that Word is a revelation of His Nature, it is first our love for the Person of Christ that should inspire our defense of the faith.

If we would not for a moment respond dispassionately or clinically to a personal attack upon our spouse, brother, sister, father, or mother, how much more so ought we be about the passionate defense of the Nature of our Lord when He is mocked by a God- and holiness-hating world?

This truth – the truth of our love for Him *personally* – should inspire matchless passion and zeal for the defense of the faith. Only through such self-sacrificial love of Him may we properly demonstrate true love and zeal for the souls of the very rebels whom we are called to diligently engage. It is only in our adoration of and submission to Christ's Nature as revealed in His Word that we are able, by His grace, to passionately, zealously defend the faith in a manner that does not go beyond the appropriate and required "offensiveness" of the Gospel and into the realm of self-righteous or hypocritical approaches that violate His Nature and contradict His Gospel.

IT'S ALL ABOUT HIM

He is the image of the invisible God, the firstborn of all creation. For by him all things were created, in heaven and on earth, visible and invisible, whether thrones or dominions or rulers or authorities—all things were created through him and for him. And he is before all things, and in him all things hold together.

CoLossians 1:15-17

Our understanding of anything at all begins with and is defined by our understanding of God. A shallow or flawed understanding of God inevitably results in a shallow or flawed understanding of His creation.

His creation is not limited to material or tangible things like water, bricks, oxygen and shoelaces. It includes every intangible or immaterial thing as well. From logic and love to oceans and kindergartners, *all* things have been made by Christ, through Christ, and for Christ (Col 1:15-17).

As such, our first task in considering the vital subject of apologetics in the life of the believer should be to approach our living, loving Lord directly, so that we might learn more about Him and, as a result, learn more about apologetics.

What could be more happy, warm, and fuzzy than that, right?

Well...

It is here that we encounter a type of problem known in strict theological terms as "a biggie". This problem is both sparked and fueled by the unhealthy combo of (A) our inherently woeful *under*estimation of God's Nature and (B) a tragically comical *over*estimation of our own. Put another way: Most of the time we tend to think of ourselves as pretty much the bee's knees, qualitatively speaking. We inherently tend to see ourselves as "good enough" to at least eek on into Heaven. This sense of perceived self-peachiness comes effortlessly and is ever so easy to sustain, so long as we test and measure ourselves *only* by the sub-biblical (meaning here *anti*-biblical) standards of man and the world. That's just how we naturally roll.

This being the case, when, by His grace, we do approach His light through the revelation of His Word and the communion of prayer, the stark reality of the juxtaposition between His holiness and our sinfulness is further illuminated with each step taken. This makes us *very* un-comfortable. We cringe. We squirm. We pretend we don't notice what He is showing us for as long as we are able, and then, again, *all by His grace*, we collapse. We are "undone", as the prophet said of himself after crying, "Woe is me!" in Isaiah 6:5. The infinite gap between God's Nature and ours is magnified in the light that is His presence. As this happens, our pride is melted away by the heat of that light, our previously unimaginable repulsiveness is made plain, and it hurts. *A lot.* So it is that we are very much inclined to run away and hide, hoping to escape that light enough to at least try to pretend again. You know, like scared, self-absorbed little kindergartners.

Yet, by His grace, He keeps His people there, in His light, so that they might not remain in the darkness of ignorance; that they might be conformed to His likeness and will.

This grace of perseverance is a gift. It may be a gift that we'd much rather *not* possess in those many shameful instances when our sinful selves desire nothing more than to run away, hide, and pretend along with the rest of this dark and dying world, but it is a gift that He will not allow His people to lose…or throw away.

He will see His people through to the end of this age and into the eternal adventure to come. He will also see His people perfectly through the brief but painful path of sanctification that they must walk in their short time in these bodies on this earth before they are fully glorified with Him in perfected new bodies on the restored earth to come. *He* will do these things, all of them, and He will do them perfectly.

These truths must be held close, and tightly so, as we consider and pursue the formation and application of a biblical apologetic, lest we forget who He is, who we are in Him, who we were apart from Him, why we are proclaiming His Gospel, and why we are defending the faith, which is an expression of His Nature.

9

A (FORGETFUL) WRETCH LIKE ME

They forgot his works and the wonders that he had shown them...

They did not remember his power or the day when he redeemed them...

PSALM 78:11 & 42

If you have detected a certain drumbeat here – a repeated theme centering on Christ's Nature as the source and explanation of *all* things, you have discerned wisely.

The reader may be pleased to know that in this relatively short book, this introduction is significantly longer than any chapter to follow. There are several reasons for this, including:

1. **The *Person* of Christ as the soul of apologetics must be apprehended** before the grand (and I do mean *grand*) truths and strategies of applied apologetics can be appreciated and deployed in a manner most glorifying to God and most beneficial to His people.

2. **We are a forgetful people.** As such, we must constantly exalt the truths of the Gospel above any of the mechanics, strategies, or tactics of what we might imagine to be "apologetics in action".

The only (and perfectly) reliable countermeasure against this forgetfulness and all of the incalculable damage it produces is the constant renewal of our minds in the Word (Romans 12:2), and He *is* the Word. *He* is where our minds must be. We are to seek *Him* diligently at all times and in all intellectual pursuits (Deut. 6:6-8), lest we be conformed to the world and submit to its standards. Only with this fundamental necessity acknowledged and embraced can we even *begin* to understand, much less pursue or practice, biblical apologetics.

PRIDE AND GRACE AND OIL AND WATER

What do you have that you did not receive? If then you received it, why do you boast as if you did not receive it?

1 CORINTHIANS 4:7

One of the things that we who have been graced with saving faith are most likely to forget is that *all things that have been given to us are, in fact and in whole, gifts from God.*

While we often accept and apply this principle to the "big things" of salvation and the like, we seem to easily forget that the same principle applies to every other thing that we've been given. Everything from our present breath and heartbeat to our knowledge and understanding of anything from tying shoelaces on up is all a gift given us through the unmerited grace of God.

If we know how to walk, that is a gift.

If we know how to speak, that is a gift.

If we know how to read, that is a gift.

If we know something of history, that is a gift.

If we are able to sing, dance, or appreciate art, these are all gifts.

Our ability to grasp logic...perceive morality...understand ethics...all are gifts.

If we have a biblical worldview, that is a gift as well.

We truly, really, and *completely* have no room to boast in ourselves (1 Cor 4:7), and when we *do* boast – which we should – we are to boast "in the Lord" (Psalm 34:2; 2 Cor 10:17) as a praise and proclamation of the great things He has chosen to do in, for, and through us for His glory and as a part of His perfect plan.

If we not only understand but *believe* this, we will behave accordingly. If we believe that everything from our ability to tie shoelaces to our understanding of theology falls under the category of "unmerited gift

11

from God", then we will not lord these gifts over others. We will strive to present their beauty in a manner that directs *all* glory to God.

Even the *desire* for any good thing is a gift in and of itself. This may seem like an obvious sort of thing to note (because it is), but we are well served to remember that the gift of a good desire is always given to us *prior* to our having it. We do not even desire the proper pursuit of language, art, history, science, or shoelace tying, until and unless He gives us that desire as a gift. When it is given, this gift comes to us while we are yet ignorant of the very thing that we are then, in an instant, graced with the desire to rightly pursue. With this in mind, it's easier to see that there is nothing inherently wrong with ignorance. *Willfully sustained* ignorance is the problem. (It's this *willful* ignorance that defines the mind and worldview of the unbeliever, as we will later explore in detail.)

So it is that we must not allow pride to prevent us from diving deep into the good things of God of which, at this moment, we may well be ignorant. We should instead thank Him for gracing us with the *recognition* of our ignorance and the *desire* to address it, as these are both gifts. If, by His grace, we are then led to a place of clarity and understanding on a particular subject, we are always to remember when sharing that beautiful new-to-us truth with others that we were once as complete in our ignorance as any other has ever been. We must never forget that it was only by the grace of God that enlightenment came our way.

Unless God gives us the desire for His will, we will not seek it; unless He guides us in the pursuit of His will, we will not find it; and unless He graces us with submission to His revealed will, we *will* rebel against it.

If you are still reading, you might well have been entertaining certain questions over the course of these first few intro pages - questions like: *"What does all of this have to do with apologetics?"* or *"When do we get to 'the good stuff', like learning how to crush an opponent in a debate?"*

Even though the second question might sound more than a tad jerky, there is a very real sense in which desiring to "destroy arguments and every lofty opinion raised against the knowledge of God" (2 Cor 10:5) is a *perfectly* honorable pursuit. Proclaiming the Gospel command and defending the faith "once for all delivered to the saints" (Jude 1:3) should be the passion of each and every believer.

Each and every one.

Each and every supernaturally reborn New Creature in Christ should, by virtue of their new Christ-centered nature, yearn to better equip themselves to defend the truth of that nature. As they pursue and cultivate a passion to defend the beauty given them, they may rest soundly in the assurance that Christ will always perfectly prepare them for this mission.

The filter being stressed here is aimed at separating the wheat from the chaff and the self-serving, debate-dominating wannabes from the Christ-centered, world-changing, personally humble soldiers of grace and the Gospel. The former bring shame and reproach to the name of Christ in pursuit of personal glory and status. The latter bring glory to the King and turn this world upside-down with the proclamation of His Gospel and the defense of His truth. May we strive for a state of constant self-examination lest we do damage to His name through our abuse of the powerful tools that He has given us to tear down enemy strongholds.

This consistent, persistent self-examination has *everything* to do with apologetics because it has everything to do with the Gospel. Our continual testing, ongoing repentance, and perpetual reformation is critical to our apologetic mission because it is central to living in light of the Gospel. It is not our mastery of techniques, tactics, philosophy or linguistics that will glorify God and win the day. It is our obedience to Him and submission to His Word that brings Him glory and brings us success as He defines it, which is the only definition that matters.

The weapons with which we have been armed are so far beyond "great" that there is not a war metaphor or analogy that could possibly come close to doing them justice. They are supernatural. They are unstoppable. The very gates of hell itself cannot withstand the Church as armed by her Lord (Matthew 16:18).

All of this is the reason for great caution, care, and self-evaluation in light of the Word.

It is in this spirit that we must prayerfully consider whether we have truly, by God's grace, embraced the faith before we can defend it. The same Lord who calls His people to His side also calls them to "count the cost" (Luke 14:25-28), "take up their cross", die to themselves, (Matthew 16:24-25) and "be crucified with Christ" (Galatians 2:20).

PEOPLE HATING (GOD'S) PEOPLE

Examine yourselves, *to see whether you are in the faith.* ***Test
yourselves****. Or do you not realize this about yourselves, that
Jesus Christ is in you?—unless indeed you fail to meet the test!*

> 2 CORINTHIANS 13:5
> (BOLD EMPHASIS ADDED)

"…**you <u>will</u> be hated** by all for my name's sake…"

> JESUS IN MATTHEW 10:22
> (EMPHASIS ADDED)

"**If the world hates you, know that it has hated me before it
hated you.** If you were of the world, the world would love you
as its own; but **because you are not of the world, but I chose
you out of the world, therefore <u>the world hates you</u>**.
Remember the word that I said to you: 'A servant is not greater
than his master.' If they persecuted me, **they <u>will</u> also
persecute you.**"

> JESUS IN JOHN 15:18-20
> (EMPHASIS ADDED)

When we understand the personal nature of Christ, His Gospel, and His
Word, as well as the personal nature of willful sin and rebellion against His
Gospel, Word, and Nature, then the use of terms like *hatred* to describe the
relationship between self-worshipping mankind and a holy God makes
sense – perfect and painfully accurate sense.

Only when the biblical presentation of the inherent hatred of *all* fallen men toward God is understood and accepted are we then in a place to coherently embrace another challenging biblical proclamation regarding the nature of man and his rebellion against holiness: *The simple, clear truth that the world **will** hate **us** for Who is in and proclaimed through us.* Our seeking to purge, by God's grace, all hypocritical judgments and self righteousness from our apologetic presentation or defense of the faith, while a good and God-glorifying pursuit, will not endear us to this world and its defenders. It will only make them hate us all the more, as true obedience always does. With this in mind, we must count the cost of that obedience (Luke 14:25-33) and embrace our cross completely.

Have we not considered the crowd that was cheering and *begging* for the crucifixion of Christ? Do we imagine that the bloodthirsty throng was composed only of *acutely* "bad people"? Were there no "kind", "generous", and "sweet" folks, as the world defines such things, howling for the death of Christ? After all, *they* hated Him too…as *they will hate us*.

The smiling, well groomed, impeccably mannered gentleman who has placed himself on the throne of his life will *hate* the obedient Christian's faithful proclamation of the Gospel. The sweet elderly lady who bakes the best cookies and gives them away with a warm, friendly smile, yet has not bent the knee in submission to Christ, will *hate* those who live in submission to Him by proclaiming His *necessity* as the center of *her* life.

It's not that we *might* be hated by these "good folk" and lovers of the world. It's not that we'll *probably* be hated by them. It's not that we will be *moderately disliked* by them. It's that we **will** be **hated** (John 15:18-20; Matthew 10:22), and this hatred will inflict great pain upon us. As the culture (temporarily) descends, the sweetest, nicest, most religious folks in the land will become some of the most vicious, vigorous persecutors of the Christians. This is the clear testimony of Scripture and history.

The time is fast coming in America and the West where it will cost His people much to faithfully proclaim His name and defend His Nature. Everything from relationships and respectability to livelihoods and lives themselves will be paid as the price of faithfulness to the King. What an honor and privilege to be one of His own in such a time as this! And how terrible for those who would "play Christian" while persecuting them.

COUNT THE COST

*Now great crowds accompanied him, and he turned and said to them, "If anyone comes to me and does not hate his own father and mother and wife and children and brothers and sisters, yes, and even his own life, he cannot be my disciple. Whoever does not bear his own cross and come after me cannot be my disciple. For which of you, desiring to build a tower, does not first sit down and count the cost, whether he has enough to complete it? Otherwise, when he has laid a foundation and is not able to finish, all who see it begin to mock him, saying, 'This man began to build and was not able to finish.' Or what king, going out to encounter another king in war, will not sit down first and deliberate whether he is able with ten thousand to meet him who comes against him with twenty thousand? And if not, while the other is yet a great way off, he sends a delegation and asks for terms of peace. So therefore, **any one of you who does not renounce all that he has cannot be my disciple**.*

Jesus (the real One) in Luke 14:25-33
(BOLD EMPHASIS ADDED)

True biblical apologetics is no plaything. It is not casual. It is not clinical. And it is anything but cheap.

To defend the faith, we must first take up our cross and follow Him through persecution, hatred from the world, and death to ourselves. We are to let go of everything this world tells us to hold dear, surrendering it all to Christ, trusting that He will give us all that we need because He has already done so in giving us Himself. Again, the personal nature of this relationship and all associated beauties is illuminated by the one-on-one reality of *Him* and *us*. We are His. He is ours. And everything, including our passion for apologetics on His terms, flows from His Nature being supernaturally imposed upon ours, allowing us to happily bear burdens that would terrify any unbeliever.

As believers by His grace, we are increasingly defined by and conformed to His Nature. As we take on more and more of His Nature, we are increasingly better equipped and more prepared for His mission. This ongoing sanctification leads us to more accurately proclaim and more faithfully apply the Gospel-fueled Great Commission, centering on His Nature as defined in His Word.

This book is written for Christians. Insofar as it is true to the Scriptures, it will not be understood by any non-believer. It will not be understood by the non-believer in these areas because it *cannot* be understood by them. Unbelievers are, by definition and as we will explore later in some depth, *incapable* of rightly understanding Scripture until and unless the Spirit of God intervenes, raising them from spiritual death unto spiritual life. This Gospel truth should inspire grace and passion in our apologetic pursuits.

Ours is a *supernatural* mission, though it is rooted in perfect logic and the perfectly coherent, objective, and *beautiful* Truth that is the *Person* of Jesus Christ.

Contrary to popular misconceptions, our adventure in apologetics does not center on the human intellect. IQ, accumulated knowledge, and the vigorous contemplation of all acquired facts to the best of one's (sometimes quite impressive) abilities are not the standards or tools by which we seek or measure success.

This is also not a mission that revolves around the freedom of one's will to pursue what it desires. All are free to choose and pursue what they desire.

This is a matter of *nature*. Nature dictates the desires of the will and therefore the freely chosen pursuits of every person ever born. All born of Adam have the fallen nature of Adam, which is a nature of rebellion against God, slavery to sin, and embrace of spiritual death. This spiritually dead nature renders their eyes, ears, mind, and *will* as incapable of accurately seeing, much less choosing, Truth. As such, there is no natural argument or apologetic, no matter how skillfully constructed or brilliantly articulated, that can or will open the eyes of those whose nature is one of happy slavery to sin and death. For dead men – and dead *minds* – to be raised to life, something *super*-natural is required.

THE GOSPEL OF GRACE

In those days John the Baptist came preaching in the wilderness of Judea, **"Repent, for the kingdom of heaven is at hand."**

MATTHEW 3:1-2
(BOLD EMPHASIS ADDED)

Now after John was arrested, Jesus came into Galilee, proclaiming the gospel of God, and saying, **"The time is fulfilled, and the kingdom of God is at hand; repent and believe in the gospel."**

MARK 1:14-15
(BOLD EMPHASIS ADDED)

The times of ignorance God overlooked, but now he commands all people everywhere to **repent, because he has fixed a day on which he will judge the world** *in righteousness by a man whom he has appointed; and of this he has given assurance to all by raising him from the dead.*

ACTS 17:30-31
(BOLD EMPHASIS ADDED)

Our aim here is to explore, adore, and apply supernaturally powerful truths rooted in the *Person* of Christ so that we might "tear down enemy strongholds" and "cast down vain imaginations" by His *personal* grace and for His *personal* glory. Whatever may come of our learning and use of these beautiful weapons against unbelievers and their worldviews, the one and only weapon that we have to raise dead men to life is the exclusive, undiluted Gospel of Jesus Christ.

Our apologetic must be defined at every turn by the whole Gospel in its full, rich, biblical context. To defend the faith is to defend the Gospel, to defend the Gospel requires sharing the Gospel, and sharing the Gospel requires us to *know* the Gospel. As such, there is no true Christian apologetic apart from explicit association with the Gospel and there are no true Christian apologists operating in a manner that is detached from the Gospel.

The nature of man as evil, the nature of God as holy, the judgment of a holy God against all evil men, and the provision of Christ as the substitutionary sacrifice paid for His people, who must and will, by His grace, heed His command to repent, believe, and be saved from His coming wrath upon all who persist in rebellion, is to always be *the* focal point of our interaction with this world. Moreover, the principles presented in the Gospel are to inform *every* aspect of our lives. Our relationships, marriages, business practices, and politics, as well as our apologetics, are to be defined by the infinite depth and beauty of the Gospel of our Lord Jesus Christ.

Far from being merely the "first step" into Christianity or gateway into deeper things, the Gospel *is* the deeper thing that must inform us in every area of life; we must seek and be reminded of it day by day, hour by hour, and moment by moment. As such, our apologetics must be *drenched* in the Gospel…lest we forget about the Nature of God, the nature of man, and the nature of salvation…lest we boast in ourselves…and lest we bring reproach upon the name and Nature of Christ.

Our passion for the defense of the faith is born of our passion for the *Person* of Jesus Christ. Our passion for others to know Him personally as their Lord and Savior ought to fuel our unrelenting presentation of His supernatural Gospel, no matter the cost.

Only *He* can make us to desire and achieve these otherwise impossible challenges, by giving Himself to us through His supernatural Gospel.

Only *He* can inspire us to happy, loving obedience.

Only *He* can inspire us to zealously defend the faith.

Only *He* can inspire us to endure any burden.

Only *He* can inspire us to do all of these things in a manner that glorifies His name.

As we move on to contemplate and explore the beauties of biblical apologetics, let us constantly remind ourselves of His Person as reflected in His Gospel. May we love Him – the *Person* of Christ – above all others and all else. May we love the lost enough to speak the truth and bring them the hope of the Gospel. And may we be graced to understand that, through all of this and every adventure we might face on this side of eternity, that it is the *Person* of Christ who is the source of all truth, life beauty, and love.

When we do these things, we will be able to build our apologetics upon *Him*. When we build our apologetics upon Him, we will then, and only then, finally be prepared to defend *His* truth on *His* terms by *His* grace and for *His* glory.

SECTION 1

IT'S ALL ABOUT HIM

"Since God is faithful to us, our apologetic must not be faithless to Him; in setting forth our defense we must not set aside or waiver with respect to the profession of our faith. Christian apologetics must begin and end with Him who is the alpha and the omega, the one who only and always reigns as Lord."

GREG L. BAHNSEN

The Alpha of Apologetics ...and Everything Else

an intro to the God who needs none

There's a popular saying: 'live and learn'. That is exactly *the first lie that Satan told Adam and Eve. . . . what God was teaching was 'learn and live'. 'Do what I tell you. You don't have to experience it, just do what I tell you. If I tell you it's good, it's good. If I say it's bad, it's bad. Trust me on this.' And then Satan comes along and says, 'No, you have to* experience *this to know whether it's right or wrong. You need to 'live and learn.'*

PAUL WASHER

We live in the age of the Precious Snowflake.

I'm a Precious Snowflake, you're a Precious Snowflake, little Johnny is a Precious Snowflake, and everybody Johnny plays with at school is, you guessed it, a unique and beautiful little Precious Snowflake of their own.

Precious Snowflakes are special. They are pure. They are good. And they are made aware of their specialness, their purity, and their goodness quite often. They are regularly and diligently reminded of their, um, *precious* qualities over and again by mommies, daddies, teachers, and McDonald's commercials. These reminders make Precious Snowflakes very happy, and, after all, isn't happy what Precious Snowflakes are supposed to be?

Precious Snowflakes are told, tell themselves, and desperately want to believe that "they can be anything that they want to be", that "they are the masters of their own destiny", and that "they deserve the best". They believe that they are the standard against which all things are to be measured and the fixed point around which all lesser but equally Precious Snowflakes are to revolve.

Lest you get the wrong notion in your not-quite-Snowflakey enough head, there is no contradiction in this. Well, there *is* contradiction in it, of course, but in the Age of Precious Snowflakes, such inconvenient rules as the law of non-contradiction are simply…gone.

Poof!

How precious is that?

What is right to one Precious Snowflake need not be right to another. What is good to one Precious Snowflake need not be good to another. What is true to one Precious Snowflake need not be true to another. There's no need to argue. No need for coherence. No need for objective standards of truth, love, logic, beauty, or anything else. I'm okay, you're okay, and we're all Precious Snowflakes.

So it is that Precious Snowflakes are also blind and stupid, but we'll get more into that later. For now, let's focus on what the Word of God tells us about the comically tragic universal human affliction known as Precious Snowflake Syndrome.

ALL KNOW GOD

*For the wrath of God is revealed from heaven against all ungodliness and unrighteousness of men, who by their unrighteousness suppress the truth. For **what can be known about God is plain to them**, because God has shown it to them. For his invisible attributes, namely, his eternal power and divine nature, have been clearly perceived, ever since the creation of the world, in the things that have been made. So they are without excuse. For although **they knew God**, they did not honor him as God or give thanks to him, but they became futile in their thinking, and their foolish hearts were darkened. **Claiming to be wise, they became fools**...*

ROMANS 1:18-22
(BOLD EMPHASIS ADDED)

All men (including all Precious Snowflakes) know God.

Not just *a* god, but *the* God. All men know *Him*. (Romans 1:19)

Not just some men, but *all* men. (Romans 1:20)

In strict theological terms, this is known as *heavy*.

It's a big deal.

And it's *very* bad news for Precious Snowflakes. This in turn makes it very unpopular everywhere that Precious Snowflake adoration is encouraged, which is another way of saying, "pretty much everywhere on earth".

Yet there He is: The Truth. And they know Him; at least enough to hate Him and be held responsible for their hatred of Him.

This is a fundamental truth of humanity on a universal scale. It is also precisely the opposite of what we, even within the church, have been led to believe and build our doctrinal, theological, and apologetic understandings upon. This is why we are well served to read, re-read, and breathe deep the crystal clear proclamation of the Word of God: *All men know Him. All men are without excuse. There is no neutral ground.*

YES, REALLY. <u>ALL</u> KNOW GOD.

*For **what can be known about God is plain to them**, because God has shown it to them. For **his invisible attributes, namely, his eternal power and divine nature, have been clearly perceived**, ever since the creation of the world, in the things that have been made. So **they are without excuse**.*

ROMANS 1:19-20
(BOLD EMPHASIS ADDED)

"Not like the fool who built his house upon the sand, the Christian apologist must, in love for Christ, found his whole life, including apologetical reasoning, upon the solid rock of *Christ's Word*."

GREG L. BAHNSEN

The first thing that we must take from Scripture on the subject of convincing anyone that God exists is that it needn't be done. It's not necessary. Ever.

Everyone knows Him. He has revealed enough about Himself so that they are without excuse for their rejection of Him. Again, how do we know this? *Because He has told us so.*

This one truth is incredibly enlightening and liberating. At the same time, it is terrifying to some and something of a lesser bummer to others.

Let's begin by addressing the "lesser bummer" category:

Back in the day, not that many years ago, a trend that had been building in my reading habits over a decade or so culminated in a torrent of Amazon.com orders that sent scads of "Christian apologetics" books to my doorstep and onto my nightstand. Truckloads (figuratively, *barely*) of good stuff on intelligent design, cosmology, microbiology, and other wonderful testimonials to the creative genius on display throughout God's

26

creation were in steady rotation in my reading line-up. I loved 'em. Still do, though in a different way; a better way. Different because I no longer view them as good baseline arguments or presentations to be aimed at unbelievers, and better because, as a believer who loves his Creator, I am able to appreciate these magnificently detailed and splendor-laden works with more appropriately focused vision. This makes me even more appreciative of these books than I had been before, *though not as primarily apologetic works.*

The important, sad, and sometimes challenging truth is that these books, as with any other compelling witness to the glory of God, are incapable of piercing the inpenetratable bubble that is Precious Snowflake Syndrome.

Only the Gospel can do that.

Of course God's matchless creativity and artistry are on vibrant display throughout His cosmos. Of course Christ's infinite beauty and splendor is reflected throughout His creation. Of course the mind of God is evidenced throughout time and space in the immutable, immaterial laws that govern His material universe. His creation has always successfully made His Nature plain to the observing image-bearers that He has placed therein, so that they are without excuse and incapable of *credibly* denying Him.

It's not a matter of evidence.

Never has been.

It's a matter of *nature*, and the nature of all Precious Snowflakes is to deny *anything* (or any *One*) that would threaten the supremacy of their own preciousness. Put another way, anything that would remove the Precious Snowflake from the throne of his or her life, or the center of his or her universe, simply is not allowed. It...is...gone.

Poof!

Remember?

Yes, *remember*.

Never forget these two central truths: 1. In Precious Snowflake Land, all things are relative and bent to the desires of the Precious Snowflake, and 2. All Precious Snowflakes, deep down in their precious, flakey little hearts, know that Precious Snowflake Land is a fiction and that God is real – not just any god, but *the* God. *We know this because He has told us so.*

DO IT FOR THE SNOWFLAKES

"To present anything less than the fullest truth of God in the name of apologetics is thoroughly sadistic."

GREG L. BAHNSEN

If we love the Snowflakes – and who doesn't? – then we will not play their game, enable their rebellion, or share in their delusion. Of infinitely greater importance, if we love the Lord Jesus Christ, we will not share or defend the Precious Snowflake's contention that they do not know God and that, consequently, His Word is proven wrong. We will affirm and stand upon the perfect truth of Scripture, rather than surrendering its clarity for the sake of appeasing the pride and ego of the Precious Snowflake.

Christ needs no introduction. He is the God known by all in His creation.

Hold this immutable truth close, Christian. It is foundational to every following chapter and every biblical apologetic principle and strategy addressed therein.

We must also never forget that we too were all born under the self-obsessive spell of Precious Snowflake Syndrome and would have eternally remained in its web had our loving Lord not seen fit to supernaturally intervene and free us from our self-focused life and the hell to follow. We were once as they are now, so...grace, grace, grace...but grace in truth, as lovingly commanded by Scripture.

When the unbeliever proclaims that "there is no God" or that they "do not know God", they...are...*lying*.

And why should this surprise us?

That's just what Precious Snowflakes do, after all. We oughta know that as former 'flakes ourselves. We also ought to know this because the God that 'flakes deny has told us so, and where the spiritually dead word of man collides with the supernaturally living Word of God...well...the man-centered side of that contest doesn't have a snowflake's chance in...

Razing Hell

One Precious Snowflake at a Time

$\Longrightarrow$

the Christian call to war on autonomy

Now the serpent was more crafty than any other beast of the field that the Lord God had made.

He said to the woman, "Did God actually say, 'You shall not eat of any tree in the garden'?" And the woman said to the serpent, "We may eat of the fruit of the trees in the garden, but God said, 'You shall not eat of the fruit of the tree that is in the midst of the garden, neither shall you touch it, lest you die.'" But the serpent said to the woman, "You will not surely die. For God knows that when you eat of it your eyes will be opened, and you will be like God . . .

GENESIS 3:1-5
(BOLD EMPHASIS ADDED)

Any decent whodunnit will feature an inquisitive protagonist asking all of the important questions: Who? What? When? Where? And *Why?*

Why was the diamond stolen, the baby kidnapped, or the car blown up?

Why was the pie poisoned, the store robbed, or the race rigged?

Why?

From Sherlock Holmes to Perry Mason, the question of motive is always a primary line of inquiry and investigation.

Where the motive of man's rebellian against and denial of God is concerned, Scripture is plain: Man rejects God's authority in pursuit of his own autonomy.

Why does man deny the God he knows to be God?

Because he so desires the façade of autonomy over the reality of God's sovreignty that he will warp, twist, and contort himself to the point that he literally abandons truth and squints his eyes in feigned denial of that which stands in the way of his imagined path to godhood. The universally dishonest denial of a knowledge of God is just as universally undertaken for the sole purpose of attempting to ascend to His throne in one's own life.

This the Precious Snowflake does in inexorable emulation of Adam before him. By virtue of his sinful nature in freely chosen action, he inevitably and quite happily trots down a path seasoned with the appealing echoes of the serpent's promise in Eden: Dismiss the one true God...disobey the one true God...pursue instead your own godhood on your own terms, and *'you will be like God'* (Genesis 3:5).

The lie of disavowing knowledge of God is the prerequestire for man's delusional pursuit of autonomy.

Just as the original lie in Eden produced immediate and terminal dysfunctionality in the relationship between the *person* of Adam and the *Person* of God, so too has every self-serving denial of God since produced the same for every descendant of Adam.

This is how hell comes to be populated with personal image-bearers of the one true and personal God. This is why we lovingly confront Precious Snowflake Syndrome with the supernatural Gospel of Jesus Christ.

LIKE FATHER, LIKE SNOWFLAKE

How you are fallen from heaven,
O Day Star, son of Dawn!
How you are cut down to the ground,
you who laid the nations low!
You said in your heart,
'I will ascend to heaven;
above the stars of God
I will set my throne on high;
I will sit on the mount of assembly
in the far reaches of the north;
I will ascend above the heights of the clouds;
I will make myself like the Most High.'

ISAIAH 14:12-14
(BOLD EMPHASIS ADDED)

Each of us when left to our inherent Precious Snowflakiness will actively and relentlessly seek to exalt ourselves as the lord or god of our own lives. We may or may not say it that way and we may or may not see it that way, but this truth is the clear testimony of Scripture. Until and unless we are liberated from self-absorption and self-exaltation through the supernatural intervention of God, we will happily, proudly, and confidently go about the business of rebellion. That's just what fallen folks do. *All* of them.

The reason for this inclination toward self-centeredness is hereditary at two levels. First, we are sons and daughters of the fallen Adam. Among other things, this means that we share in Adam's sinful, fallen nature. Adam's sin of rebellion was born of his prideful desire to be the lord of his own life. Adam's sin was the prideful pursuit of *autonomy*.

It is the desired autonomy (rebellion) of the human heart that paints all actions inspired by it as sinful. Here again, by "all actions" we mean *all* actions, including, but not limited to: Reading, writing, thinking, dancing,

31

baking cookies, and…well…any otherwise lawful and "good" thing that a person might do. Even the "plowing of the field" by the wicked, unrepentant man is sin (Proverbs 21:4 KJV).

And why is it sin?

Because it is separated from the Person of Christ through the pursuit of *autonomy*.

The pursuit of autonomy, which is by definition the rejection of the lordship of the Person of Christ in favor of the lordship of the person of self, inherently and completely corrupts *anything* to which it is attached. *Everything* done in a spirit of autonomy is sin.

This universally destructive desire for autonomy leads nicely into our consideration of the second manner in which we have inherited our sinful nature and desires. The very notion of autonomy was first planted in us – into our very nature – by the spiritual father of autonomy himself: Satan.

The father of rebellion against the authority of God is described again and again in Scripture as the father of those who join in his wicked pursuit of pride-fueled, self-exalting autonomy.

Scripture is very hard and very clear where the nature of *all* unrepentant rebels is concerned. If the term "Precious Snowflake" sounds a bit snarky, harsh, or edgy, and you fear that speaking of those who pursue self over God in such a manner crosses the line of propriety, try using, or at least *contemplating*, some of these *biblical* tags:

- **Slave to sin** (Romans 6:17).
- **Hater of God** (Romans 1:30).
- **Hater of Christ** (John 15:18-20).
- **Hater of Christians** (Matthew 10:22).
- **Child of wrath** (Ephesians 2:3).
- **Child of the devil** (1 John 3:10).

Remember first and always as you read and (hopefully) re-read the above list: *This was **me** before He saved me*. Each and every one of these terrible, brutal, and utterly *true* descriptions of *all* unrepentant unbelievers once applied just as completely to *us* as they now do to anyone else. *We* were slaves to sin, and not in the sense you may be thinking. We *loved* our bondage. We *loved* our chains. We *loved* our sin and we *hated* holiness. *That's* how utterly enslaved *we* were, and would still be, were it not for the grace of God saving us while we still hated Him.

People understandably love and are encouraged to "write in their name" where the promises of God are presented in Scripture, so that passages like Romans 8:28 might be taken more *personally*.

This can be a good thing and a source of encouragement for the true believer, but our selective application of this "write a name in" approach is very telling. We aren't very much inclined to "write names" into the passages that describe the condition of all unbelievers ever born, and we are *especially* hesitant to make personal application of what the bible proclaims as truth regarding unbelievers that we like or follow or generally think highly of. This denial of the clearly revealed truth of human nature stifles our Gospel presentation and warps our worldview from something biblical to something worldly. From that secularized, autonomy enabling position, we help the father of lies, including the lie of autonomy, to populate hell with the souls of the lost.

Thus the nature and purpose of the devil is realized in his children and often accommodated by the professing church. In our aversion to biblical truth regarding the nature of man we enable the expansion of the very hell that we've been called and equipped to destroy (Matthew 16:17-19).

The Gospel cannot be credibly, coherently proclaimed where the nature of man is soft-peddled or denied.

We hated God. *We* hated Christ. *We* hated Christians. *We* were children of wrath. *We were children of the devil.*

As we were, the lost are now.

If we love our Lord, and if we love the lost, we will not shrink from these brutal but essential truths. If we love our Lord and we love the lost, we will proclaim the vivid, detailed, and challenging truth of John 8: 34-45, which reads:

> *Jesus answered them, "Truly, truly, I say to you, everyone who practices sin is a slave to sin. The slave does not remain in the house forever; the son remains forever. So if the Son sets you free, you will be free indeed. I know that you are*

*offspring of Abraham; yet you seek to kill me because my word finds no place in you. **I speak of what I have seen with <u>my Father</u>, and you do what you have heard from <u>your father</u>.***"

*They answered him, "Abraham is our father." Jesus said to them, "If you were Abraham's children, you would be doing the works Abraham did, but **now you seek to kill me**, a man who has told you the truth that I heard from God. This is not what Abraham did. **You are doing the works <u>your father</u> did.**" They said to him, "We were not born of sexual immorality. We have one Father—even God." Jesus said to them, "If God were your Father, you would love me, for I came from God and I am here. I came not of my own accord, but he sent me. Why do you not understand what I say? It is because you **<u>cannot</u>** bear to hear my word. **You are of <u>your father the devil</u>, and your will is to do <u>your father's desires</u>.** He was a murderer from the beginning, and does not stand in the truth, because there is no truth in him. When he lies, he speaks out of his own character, for he is a liar and the father of lies. But **because I tell the truth, you do not believe me.***

John, known to many as "The Apostle of Love", is supposed to be the "warm and gentle" one of the bunch, yet it is clear from the above passage that his understanding of what is loving has little in common with the contemporary understanding (or self-serving redefinition) of the term. "The Apostle of Love" also said the following in 1 John 3:8-10:

*The reason the Son of God appeared was to destroy the works of the devil. No one born of God makes a practice of sinning, for God's seed abides in him, and he cannot keep on sinning because he has been born of God. **By this it is evident who are the <u>children of God</u>, and who are the <u>children of the devil</u>:** whoever does not practice righteousness is not of God, nor is the one who does not love his brother.*

Are we seeing the picture here? Are we even *willing* to see it?

If so on either count, it is only so by the grace of God. Remember: *Everything* is a gift.

The picture of fallen humanity's default nature as painted by John is as vivid as the beautiful portrait he was inspired to craft of the Lord Himself in his Gospel. John passionately portrayed the Person of Christ as the exclusive source of every good thing, and, as such, the necessary *Person* to whom all other persons must submit in order to have access to any good thing. These truths are at the core of Christianity's beauty and autonomy's horror.

When a man, *any* man, persists in autonomy, *he does so willfully and with specific awareness of the one true God he aims to displace*. This is the clear truth revealed in Romans 1 and explored in some detail in the previous chapter. Holding that truth about man's knowledge of God in one hand, the truth about the nature of autonomy in the other, and bringing the two together in their biblical context will help us to understand many important things, including:

1. **Autonomy is the *personal* rejection of the *Person* of Christ.**

2. **As such, the desire for autonomy makes *every* subsequent pursuit *sinful*.**

3. **Hell is the ultimate, and proper, destination for all who are driven by the desire for autonomy.**

When we understand that *all* who seek to live autonomously are *personally* rejecting the God that they know, that their autonomous lives can *only* produce sinful actions, and that we were once as they are now until Christ saved us through His Gospel, we are in a much better place to appreciate, adore, and proclaim that Gospel, and happily so, no matter the cost in this world.

Remember: Before a Precious Snowflake can be saved, it *must* be convicted and led to repent, which is almost always preceded by being offended. *Deeply* offended. Only the Gospel can inspire such offense, conviction and repentance, as nobody should know better than believers, all of whom are themselves former 'flakes saved by grace.

Raising (and Annoying) the Dead

lovingly proclaiming the most hated of truths

*Therefore, if anyone is in Christ, he is a new creation. The old has passed away; behold, the new has come. All this is from God, who through Christ reconciled us to himself and **gave us the ministry of reconciliation***; *that is, in Christ God was reconciling the world to himself, not counting their trespasses against them, and **entrusting to us the message of reconciliation***. *Therefore, **we are ambassadors for Christ, God making his appeal through us. We implore you on behalf of Christ, be reconciled to God.***

2 Corinthians 5:17-20
(Bold emphasis added)

The whole, undiluted Gospel of Jesus Christ is the most offensive, repulsive, and hated message ever to hit the ears of mankind. Just ask Joel Osteen.

The whole truth of the Gospel is a secular marketer's worst nightmare. It is a secular marketer's worst nightmare because *it is the secular world's worst nightmare*. Practically everything upon which modern American and Western culture has been built over the past century is diametrically opposed to each and every core proclamation of the Gospel of Jesus Christ.

This is where the "hatred of the world" test discussed earlier really comes in handy (see: John 15:18-20). Any way we slice it and from any angle we approach it, our willingness (or unwillingness) to personally share the whole, hated Gospel of the Person of Jesus Christ with those pursuing autonomy (rebellion) all around us is the dividing line between the only two camps of humanity:

1. **Those who love God, love the lost, and hate worldliness, as *all three are defined biblically*,**

   and

2. **Those who love self more than God, love self more than the lost, and defend worldliness against the truth of Scripture when the former is offended by the latter.**

Should we test ourselves this way in light of Scripture, the results may well be convicting.

This conviction is a gift, remember?

When it comes, thank God for it, repent, and grow, by His grace and for His glory. That same Gospel answer is the only path to true, ongoing peace and "abundant life" for both the believer and the unbeliever alike. Both camps need the Gospel, and desperately so.

This is why the one camp in whom the Gospel has been made alive ought to be inspired to share that life at every opportunity with the camp that is, at present, destined for the eternal darkness of autonomy.

THEOLOGY MATTERS

"The Gospel is ours to proclaim, not to edit."

JAMES WHITE

"As God makes a total demand upon the lives of His covenant people they recognize that the words of Scripture are logically primitive, the most ultimate authority."

GREG L. BAHNSEN

Christian theology and Christian doctrine are reflections of the *Person* of Christ. They are from and a part of Him. They are portrait of who He is. So it is that seeking and embracing the most challenging details of His revelation of Himself through His Word is something we must pray for the grace and desire to pursue with all the passion that our earthbound hearts and bodies can hold.

As Christian theology is a presentation of the very personhood of Christ, it is essential to our apologetic cause. We must guard diligently against the temptation to slide into man-centered theology or allow a man-centered apologetic desire for the salvation of the lost to displace a God-centered theological foundation that measures success not by numbers of professed conversions, but by complete obedience to the Word of God and the faithful presentation of the Gospel given therein.

It's all about Him: The Person of Christ.

The more of Him that we can know and embrace, the better. The more of Him that we choose to dismiss or ignore in favor of our own autonomous determinations as to what is good, true, or beautiful, the more we, even as believers, invite darkness and death into our lives and culture. While the sin-enslaved world of pagans has their own spiritual blindness as an excuse for such a worldview, we do not. We have no excuses. We are completely accountable to the Christ we proclaim as Lord in ways that they are not, for when we sin and surrender His revelation in favor of our own autonomy, we do so after having been given eyes to see better. In so doing, we mock the Lord who has saved us.

Even so, when conviction of this truth comes to us, as it is likely to do time and time again, it is a gift. It is a gift to be followed by another gift: Repentance. And then another: Restoration. This is the Gospel in action in the life of the believer, and this is the Gospel that we are lovingly commanded to take to a world filled with sinners who are perishing in pursuit of autonomy.

Contrary to the guiding principles of the present age, the feelings of Precious Snowflakes are not the most important things in the universe. They're not even the most important things to the Precious Snowflake, though you'd never convince them of it. The most important thing to the Precious Snowflake is the same thing that is most important to the believer: The Person of Jesus Christ – the Person rejected by the 'flake and embraced by the believer through the Gospel of that very same Person.

In the next section, we will explore some of the extraordinary measures and tools employed by the Precious Snowflake in his rejection of the Person of Christ. So buckle up, take a deep breath, pray for nausea suppression, and get ready to take stroll through the spiritual and intellectual wasteland known as...*autonomy*.

SECTION 2

THE TOOLS OF FOOLS
Cherished Mythologies of the Willful Idiot

"The options are God and absurdity, and people choose absurdity because they love their sin."

SYE TENBRUGGENCATE

Swiss Cheesiness

><>

the myth of neutrality

*For **what can be known about God is plain to them**, because God has shown it to them. For **his invisible attributes, namely, his eternal power and divine nature, have been clearly perceived**, ever since the creation of the world, in the things that have been made. So **they are without excuse**.*

ROMANS 1:19-20
(BOLD EMPHASIS ADDED)

"**Whoever is not with me is against me**, and whoever does not gather with me scatters."

JESUS IN MATTHEW 12:30
(BOLD EMPHASIS ADDED)

Our autonomy worshipping pop culture, as an unintended witness to its intellectual vapidity, is routinely about the business of rolling out mind-numbingly stupid proclamations of what it imagines to be profound "truth".

Take Jedi Knight Obi-Wan Kenobi, for example. In *Star Wars Episode III: Revenge of the Sith*, Obi-Wan, when addressed by his nemesis (a sharp dressing up-and-comer named Darth Vader) with the proclamation that those who are "not with me are against me", responds with this colossal gem of oxymoronic idiocy: "Only the Sith deal in absolutes."

For those of you not up to speed on *Star Wars* lore, "the Sith" of which Obi-Wan spoke are the baddest of the bad guys in *Star Wars* land – the embodiment of evil. And, apparently, only *they* deal in absolutes.

Whether Kenobi even realized that his response could be taken as his way of coming out as a Sith or not is a discussion for another time. Assuming that the intent of Obi-Wan's comeback was *not* to proclaim his heretofore secret Sithiness, he is then guilty of a glaringly self-contradicting statement – a pronouncement that, by the time it finishes rolling out of one's mouth, has already disproven the point it was trying to make in the first place. This, in strict linguistic terms, is known as "really dumb".

Professing atheists tend to do this kind of thing all the time.

'Cause they have to.

It's all they've got.

"There are no absolutes!" is the never-ending nonsensical battlecry of many of those whom Scripture describes as willful idiots or "fools". So entranced are these fools by the pursuit of autonomous rule over their lives that they are blinded from noticing even the most egregious of logical bloopers as they roll one after another after another off their tongues and out of their mouthes…again and again as unintended acknowlegments of their intellectual vacancy and *foolishness*.

The myth of neutrality is one of the most cherished myths of the fool who says in his heart that "there is no God" (Psalm 14:1). It should not be the least little bit surprising that this myth is easily exposed as fiction by the light of Scripture. Our aim as believers is to embrace Scripture's proclamation on this matter and **never let it go** – never surrender this fact, even in the face of the loudest, boldest, most passionate proclamations of protestation emanating from…the *fool* who *hates* the God that they *know*.

If we love the fool, that Precious Snowflake, we will *not* play his game. We will *not* agree with his biblically impossible-to-believe claim. We will *not* surrender the authority of the crystal clear Word of God in order to somehow then inch the unbeliever towards belief in the authority of that same Word. Such an approach would be every bit as idiotic as the Obi-Wan quote mentioned earlier, and we don't wanna go there, do we?

HELPING THE FOOL
(BY CONFRONTING HIS FOOLISHNESS)

"If you start with the neutrality of reason as your premise, you have no way, legitimately, to bring in another authority that grounds that reasoning process. That becomes the problem."

K. SCOTT OLIPHINT

*The **fool** says in his heart, "There is no God."*
They are corrupt, they do abominable deeds,
there is none who does good.

PSALM 14:1
(BOLD EMPHASIS ADDED)

The *fool* denies the God he knows because that God has spoken authoritatively against the manner in which the fool desires to live. The fool utterly rejects the authority of the Word, as it constantly condemns the self-centered desires of men who are determined to do things and live life in their own way and on their own terms…also known as, you guessed it, the pursuit of *autonomy*. Autonomy is all about the authority of the individual. Christianity is all about the authority of God over everyone, and the authoruty of His Word as the perfect, sufficient revelation as to what that means in every area of life.

CONFRONTING THE REBEL'S DARK (AND DUMB) PRESUPPOSITIONS

"Since neutrality is unattainable for either the unbeliever or believer, and since they have conflicting ultimate standards for judging claims to knowledge, the task of apologetics will ultimately be carried on at the presuppositional level."

GREG L. BAHNSEN

When we play along with the fool's contention that they "don't know God", which is born of the presupposition that God is **not** known to all men, we are joining them in their rejection of the authority of Scripture.

We are validating their contention.

We are playing the fool.

Or the Precious Snowflake.

Or some other similarly awful thing (feel free to revisit the list of six biblical tags for unbelievers presented in Chapter Two).

Neutrality is a fiction. It does not exist.

How do we know this?

Because God has told us so in His Word.

When we embrace this truth, we honor the Person of Christ, whose Nature we are defending. In doing so we position ourselves to better understand and confront the many other cherished myths of the unbeliever in a manner that brings glory to God, growth to His people, and, Lord willing, the expansion of His Kingdom through the supernatural salvation of souls.

Daddy (Isn't There) Issues

$\prec\!\!\!\prec\!\!\!\Longrightarrow$

the myth of autonomy

And since they did not see fit to acknowledge God, God gave them up to a debased mind...

ROMANS 1:28

"The options are God and absurdity, and people choose absurdity because they love their sin."

SYE TENBRUGGENCATE

There he hung, dangling on the edge of a seemingly bottomless pit that had just opened beneath him, holding onto life with his right hand and reaching down into the darkness with his left.

"Junior, give me your other hand! I can't hold on!"

"I can get it," he responded almost to himself under his breath. His focus and left hand's fingers were fixed on the shiney object of undivided affection laying just below him in the pit, just out of reach, but so tantalizingly close. He could literally feel it with the tip of his fingers.

"I can almost reach it, dad," he continued with conviction and anxiety born of the intense hope and desire that had overtaken him as he stretched and stretched and...

"Indiana."

The voice from above was calm and clear this time. It's clarity pierced the fog that had come over the man hanging on the edge of oblivion. It brought an awareness that had been lost in pursuit of the treasure that was just...out of...reach.

"*Indiana*."

This time the voice was even more purposeful. It was pleading, but in a calm, controlled manner.

"Let it go."

And with that, Indiana Jones came to his senses, abandoned the Holy Grail that a moment before had him reaching for death, and obeyed his loving father's call, who then lifted him from the pit.

This magical movie moment from *Indiana Jones and the Last Crusade* is rich. It speaks powerfully to the self-destructive practice of idolatry.

In this particular Hollywood adventure, Indiana and his father, the elder professor Henry Jones, were both captivated by the lure of the Holy Grail. Its splendor entranced the senior Jones throughout much of his academic career. Its physical reality nearly cost the younger Jones his life in the cavernous pit that ultimately took the Grail from them both, swallowing it into the darkness that would have also snatched young Indiana, but for the purposeful, life-saving words of his loving father.

Idols and idolatry are part and parcel of fallen human nature. As Calvin rightly noted, "the human heart is a perpetual factory of idols."

In the heirarchy of idolotry, autonomy is at the pinnacle. It is the form fitting glove to the fleshly hand of pride, the first and favorite idol of the fallen human heart.

Autonomy is fallen man's mastering mirage.

It is his Holy Grail. It is his *Precious*.

IMPOSSIBILITY + INSANITY = AUTONOMY

*He is the image of the invisible God, the firstborn of all creation. For by him all things were created, in heaven and on earth, **visible and invisible**, whether thrones or dominions or rulers or authorities—**all things were created through him and for him. And he is before all things, and in him all things hold together**.*

COLOSSIANS 1:15-17
(EMPHASIS ADDED)

*. . . Christ, **in whom** are hidden **all** the treasures of wisdom and knowledge*.

COLOSSIANS 2:2-3
(EMPHASIS ADDED)

God the Spirit through Paul in his letter to the Colossians could not have been more plain: *Each and every thing was created through the Person of Jesus Christ for the Person of Jesus Christ*. In context, the "all things" of Colossians 1:15-17 really, truly does mean *all things*. Everything from law, economics, and love to religion, sexuality, and the bird chirping in an apartment complex tree was made *through* the Person of Jesus Christ and *for* the Person of Jesus Christ.

Later in the letter, a corresponding truth is proclaimed when in Colossians 2:2-3, we learn that "all the treasures of wisdom and knowledge" are hidden in the Person of Jesus Christ. They are a part of Him. His Nature produces, defines, and sustaines them. *There is **no** knowledge and there is **no** wisdom to be found apart from His Person*. He *is* Truth (John 14:6).

So when someone asks or ponders the question, "What is truth?" the answer is Jesus Christ. To deny Christ is to deny truth, knowledge, and wisdom. As these things are impossible apart from Him, all that can be left to the unbeliever is the insanity of a truth-less, knowledge-less existence.

That insanity is always the unavoidable consequence of autonomy, since autonomy's aim is to separate one from the authority and Nature of the living, *personal* source of all knowledge and wisdom.

AUTONOMY'S SLAVES

*Jesus answered them, "Truly, truly, I say to you, **everyone who practices sin is a slave to sin**.*

JOHN 8:34
(BOLD EMPHASIS ADDED)

It's important to remember that to the spiritually blind, dead, and sin-enslaved mind, autonomy is as real as any mirage has ever been to any man desperate for the sight of that which they wished was really there. To the unbeliever, their self-delusion is so great that autonomy *is* there…it's *within reach*…it is utterly *attainable*. They can see it. They can *taste* it.

In their burning desire for sin they will not surrender the notion of autonomous rule over their own life, their minds become more and more warped, and their senses become increasingly distorted over time. They will deny any objective standard or truth, *no matter the evidence* and *no matter the experience of consequences related to their denials*. They will *never* surrender their pursuit of autonomy.

They will reach for that unattainable mirage of an idol with all that they have. They will, if left to themselves, spend their every thought and every breath in its pursuit.

It is their identity.

It is their everything.

It *owns* them.

How's that for irony?

Autonomy owns its worshippers in that it literally defines *everything* they think or do. As we find in Scripture, the separation of any thing from the Person of Jesus Christ renders that thing hideous, lifeless, truthless, and destructive. For the sin-perverted mind, however, this is a price worth paying. As insane as that sounds, it is so nonetheless.

The would-be autonomous man can and will sacrifice everything, including truth, logic, morality, and even sanity itself, to fuel the blind rage and hatred that he has for the Father.

DADDY (AND AUTHORITY) ISSUES

*Children, **obey your parents in the Lord**, for this is right. "Honor your father and mother" (this is the first commandment with a promise), "that it may go well with you and that you may live long in the land."*

EPHESIANS 6:1-3
(BOLD EMPHASIS ADDED)

The essence of autonomy is the rejection of any personal authority over one's self. That being the case, it shouldn't be the least bit surprising to us that a people increasingly in pursuit of absolute autonomy would experience increasing dysfunction at the family level. The rejection of God the Father as the adored, respected, and ruling Head over humanity is mirrored in rebellious man's propensity to rebel against any and every father figure placed before him.

Just as the pouting, undisciplined, self-obsessed child screams and rages in disobedience, so too does the "adult" unbeliever pout and rail against the Father he knows is there…and hates.

This is not mere rhetorical pounding against the unbeliever; it's an important and foundational reality of his nature and worldview. We are well served to note this ugly truth as we form a biblically coherent understanding of fallen man and a biblically faithful apologetic to defend the faith from that man…all with the hope that the Gospel may be used by the Father to raise the pouting, childish, would-be autonomous ruler from spiritual darkness and death to abundant and eternal life.

However much fallen man may wish or imagine or delude himself into believing otherwise, *autonomy is a fiction*. It does not exist.

How do we know this?

Because God has told us so in His Word.

Every single breath, thought, bit of logic, and use of language employed by the wannabe autonomous, self-ruling Precious Snowflake is *completely dependant upon the Person of Christ*. It is a gift…a gift by the unmerited grace of the very God they hate. The more clearly we understand and present this truth, the better.

6

Precious Snowflake Syndrome

~~><>

the myth of innocence

*...all, both Jews and Greeks, are under sin, as it is written:
"None is righteous, no, not one; no one understands; no one
seeks for God. All have turned aside; together they have
become worthless; no one does good, not even one."*

*Their throat is an open grave; they use their tongues to
deceive. The venom of asps is under their lips. Their mouth is
full of curses and bitterness. Their feet are swift to shed blood;
in their paths are ruin and misery, and the way of peace they
have not known. There is no fear of God before their eyes."*

*Now we know that whatever the law says it speaks to those
who are under the law, so that every mouth may be stopped,
and the whole world may be held accountable to God. For by*

works of the law no human being will be justified in his sight, since through the law comes knowledge of sin.

*But now the righteousness of God has been manifested apart from the law, although the Law and the Prophets bear witness to it—the righteousness of God through faith in Jesus Christ for all who believe. For there is no distinction: for **all have sinned and fall short of the glory of God**...*

ROMANS 3:9-23
(BOLD EMPHASIS ADDED)

Remember the Precious Snowflakes?

How could we forget.

After all...we were once in that very precious club ourselves, painful though that past reality may be to recall.

At any rate, in light of the truths we've embraced and the myths we've exposed thus far, one thing should already be very clear: Biblical truth is brutal on the Snowflakes. It exposes their cherished myths as fiction and confronts them with the very truths that they are desperately trying to avoid by way of autonomy.

Both the Snowflake's cherished myths of personal neutrality (discussed in Chapter Four) and personal innocence are natural byproducts of their imagined state of autonomy. The Snowflake's perceived innocence, which entitles him to the claim of neutrality, is made possible only by the elimination of the personal authority of Christ through the imposition of autonomy, which removes Jesus from the throne of judgment and replaces Him with *self.* Put another way, the Snowflake, by claiming autonomous rule over his own life by his own standards, imagines himself to be the naturally good and proper judge of all things, able to assess them from what he imagines to be a fair and capable neutral position, all due to his inherent, original, and somehow preservable *innocence.*

As the Snowflake sees things, he really does begin and is able to continue through life as something at least roughly as pure as the wind-driven snow. Contrary to Scripture (Psalm 51:5; Romans 3:9-23), he believes that he is born innocent.

Even more tragically, he often imagines himself to *remain* in that state.

54

DECEITFUL ABOVE ALL THINGS

*The heart is **deceitful above all things**,*
*and **desperately sick**;*

JEREMIAH 17:9
(EMPHASIS ADDED)

While everything from billboards and chick flicks to power ballads and even many "preachers" partake in promoting the cultural drumbeat that encourages us all to "listen to our heart", it really shouldn't surprise us all that much to find that the perfect, personal Word from our living, loving Lord has *precisely the opposite* advice. He describes the human heart as *deceitful above all things, utterly untrustworthy,* and *desperately sick* (Jeremiah 17:9). While we may not find that sentiment sprinkled onto many contemporary top-forty hits – even on "Christian radio", we ought to find it playing a significant role in the foundation of our worldview and worldview in action (also known as *our lives*).

In the book of Romans, God the Spirit through the Apostle Paul meticulously and methodically makes the case against *all* of humanity, bringing a righteous, *universal* indictment against *every* man, woman, boy, and girl born with the self-referential nature of Adam. He makes it plain that *we are **all** born under sin* (Romans 3:9), that ***none or us** are righteous* (3:11), that ***none of us** naturally seek after God* (3:11), and that ***none of us**, as a result of our naturally sinful, "autonomous", self-focused insanity, even do good things* as God measures such things (3:12).

So much for the worldview of the Precious Snowflake.

By looking away from the Person of God in Eden, and looking instead to the person of self as the judge of truth, Adam embraced the mirage of autonomy. As such, he, and everyone born after him with his nature as their own, is naturally enslaved to the insanity of their own logically, morally, and *literally* baseless *self*-exalting worldview. They are born with a love for autonomy and a hatred for the God who stands in its way.

THE BUBBLE WORLD OF UNBELIEF

"Everyone then who hears these words of mine and does them will be like a wise man who built his house on the rock. And the rain fell, and the floods came, and the winds blew and beat on that house, but it did not fall, because it had been founded on the rock. And **everyone who hears these words of mine and does not do them will be like a foolish man who built his house on the sand.** And the rain fell, and the floods came, and the winds blew and beat against that house, and it fell, and great was the fall of it."

JESUS IN MATTHEW 7:24-27
(BOLD EMPHASIS ADDED)

The unbeliever's worldview is a very tender "reality".

It is fragile.

It is weak.

It is *foolish*.

It is all of these things because it has no solid foundation; no undergirding, objective basis for...well...*anything*. It is the quintessential "house built on sand" described in Matthew 7:24-27 because the foundation of *all things*, the Person of Christ, has been rejected in favor of a foundation capable of supporting absolutely *nothing*: the self.

This tender, fragile, foolish little house on the sand may often be cloaked in the *appearance* of proud, confident invulnerability and inpenetrable toughness, but that veneer is see-through, trace-paper thin when examined through the lense of a true biblical worldview. The big talking, proudly strutting Precious Snowflake on the other side of that facade of self-confidence is just one sharp poke away from seeing his bubbleworld pop, leaving him to plunge into just the sort of desperation one would expect from a man whose whole world quickly collapses around him.

It is our job to pop that bubble (see: 2 Corinthians 10:5).

That's what obedient Christians who truly love the lost do to Truth-denying bubbleworlds that captivate and can only lead unbelievers to eternal darkness. Of course, our acting in such a manner will not often endear us to anyone beside the King of the Universe and His people.

Oh wait.

That's pretty good, isn't it?

Even so, every God-hating rebel in a world of God-hating rebels will hate us for our purposefully trying to pop their autonomy-fueled theological, philosophical, ethical, economic, and moral bubbles. This is why we ought to spend much time, thought, and prayer counting the cost of what we're doing when we embrace the Person of Christ by taking up our cross and following Him in His Gospel-fueled Great Commission.

When we obey Him and bring what amounts to an unstoppable, nuclear-powered, enormous wrecking-ball swinging, worldview obliterating machine to the previously happy little bubble worlds of 'Flakeville, those bubbles *will* pop, Precious Snowflakes *will* melt down in their exposure, and we *will* be savagely, viciously attacked from *all* sides not grounded in the Person of Christ.

Yet make no mistake: If we truly love our Lord and the lost, that is *exactly* what we will do, on *His* terms and by *His* grace, *with gentleness and respect.*

GENTLENESS, RESPECT, AND WARFARE

*For though we walk in the flesh, we are not waging war according to the flesh. For the weapons of our warfare are not of the flesh but have divine power to destroy strongholds. **We destroy arguments and every lofty opinion raised against the knowledge of God, and take every thought captive to obey Christ**...*

2 CORINTHIANS 10:3-5
(BOLD EMPHASIS ADDED)

*...in your hearts honor Christ the Lord as holy, **always being prepared to make a defense to anyone who asks you** for a reason for the hope that is in you; **yet do it <u>with gentleness and respect</u>**...*

1 PETER 3:15

(EMPHASIS ADDED)

So how exactly is one able to be "gentle" in use of an unstoppable, nuclear-powered, enormous wrecking-ball swinging, worldview obliterating machine to destroy the many happy little bubble worlds of 'Flakeville?

By keeping our eyes on the *Person* of Christ as revealed perfectly in His Word.

In so doing, by His grace we will be inspired to hate what He hates and love what He loves, presenting His truth on His terms in a Spirit that adds nothing in the area of personal offense that is not already inherent in the most personally offensive message ever brought to men: The Gospel.

While there are many good and useful things that could be said and beneficial steps that could be prescribed, all aimed at guiding believers toward a proper approach to Christ-centered, God-honoring warfare of the like described in 2 Corinthians 5, the simplest and best thing that we can do is pray and test ourselves – our spirits, motives, and desires - in the perfect light of Scripture.

Do we use terms like "haters of God", "Children of the devil" or "Precious Snowflakes" as painful but true descriptive tools with which to properly portray the unmatched folly and eternal consequences of the self-centered worldview of "autonomous" rebels precariously positioned on the precipice of hell? Or do we use these terms as a hammer with which to mock and pound them into puddles of defeated rage because, while they may indeed hate God, we actually hate *them*?

Do we proclaim the Gospel command to repent to autonomy lovers out of a desperate, passionate desire for them to heed that command because we have a burning love for their eternal souls, each of which uniquely bears the image of the Lord we love *even more* and Who loved us enough to suffer the wrath of God on our behalf, while *we* hated *Him*? Or do we issue the Gospel command out of a desire for the unbeliever's hellbound worldview to be realized, sending them into eternal judgment and darkness, because we desire their punishment more than we desire their salvation?

These are the questions we must ask ourselves. These are the tests we should take, and often.

As defenders of the faith, every Christian is to be about the task of tearing down enemy strongholds and destroying worldviews that exalt themselves against the knowledge of God. That is our mission. If we are truly in Christ, we will pursue that mission as He has defined it, with gentleness and respect, as He has defined them.

We cannot allow the myth of human innocence to stand. Human innocence is a fiction. It does not exist.

How do we know this?

Because God has told us so in His Word.

If we love our Lord and love the lost, self-centered rebels who hold the myth of human innocence near and dear to their stoney hearts, and we desire those hearts to be made alive through the Gospel, we will confront them with the truth of their guilt, before a holy God. What less could we desire as former Precious Snowflakes ourselves who have, by that same Gospel power, been graced with conviction, repentance, belief, and salvation?

Stupid Pagan Tricks

~~><>

the impossibility of non-Christian worldviews

*The fear of the Lord is the **beginning** of knowledge;*
fools despise wisdom and instruction.

PROVERBS 1:7

The fool says in his heart, "There is no God."
They are corrupt, doing abominable iniquity;

PSALM 53:1

*Answer not a **fool** according to his folly,*
  lest you be like him yourself.
*Answer a **fool** according to his folly,*
  lest he be wise in his own eyes.

PROVERBS 26:4-5

(EMPHASIS ADDED TO EACH OF THE ABOVE THREE PASSAGES)

"Oh man! Don't *even* bring that into my house!"

I remember saying those words and rolling my eyes on the fateful mid-'90s night as if it happened yesterday. My friend Jim had called ahead to tell me about a video that I just *had* to see. I was more than a bit curious and interested by the time he made it to my door about an hour later, video in hand.

Then I saw the cover and my mind flashed a familiar warning; a warning I like to call the "I Must Never Watch Professional Wrestling" alert.

The cover of the video had set off the alarm I'd programmed and enabled long ago for self-preservation purposes. There was some cartoony figure flexing his arms, looking ridiculous in a very pro wrestling-ish way. The title of the video didn't help things any. It only made the siren in my head sound louder.

The Ultimate Fighting Championship...II!

Oh man!

About two seconds into my eyes scanning the video cover, I was thinking, "What is Jim thinking?" Apparently, he could tell that was what I was thinking.

"No! I know! But you have to see this! It's real!"

Like I hadn't heard *that* one a gajillion times before from wrestling fans. But this was Jim. Jim knew me. He knew me well. So I let him in...with the video.

What followed on that night was one of those transformative moments that you thank God for and never forget. Really.

First off, and most importantly, it was *real* – an honest-to-goodness, no-holds-barred, full-contact martial arts tournament.

Not only was it a real tournament, but it was wide-open in that there were sixteen guys at the start, randomly matched against each other for round one of the tourney. There were no weight classes. There were no style-based categories. There were only like one or two rules.

There were also only four ways to win these fights and advance to the next round (which would follow on the same night, by the way):

1. Knock out your opponent.
2. Submit your opponent (which involved him "tapping out", usually before passing out and/or having a limb or joint broken).

3. Having the referee stop the fight.
4. Having your opponent's corner throw in the towel.

There were no time limits. There were no rounds. There were no judges, and therefore no scorecard decisions. As you might imagine, this "realistic-as-possible" tourney brought out some interesting characters.

There were some lean, mean, kickboxing machines; there were 250 pound-ish Judo masters; there were Gaston-esque physiqued shoot-fighting champions, and then there was…Royce Gracie.

Royce rolled into the event at 6'1" and about a buck seventy-five. He wasn't particularly muscular in appearance and not overly lean. He was lean enough alright and in excellent shape, don't get me wrong, but he was clearly not one of those 1% body fat folks that we see so much of in the pro sports world these days. He was unassuming, polite, soft spoken, and anything but intimidating. He didn't even seem to have particularly good posture.

When he would walk into the middle of the octagon (the martial-artsy, eight-sided take on a "ring") to meet his opponent, he looked *so* chill. Way too relaxed. He was even slouched just enough under his gi (the white robe/uniform of many a martial artist) that I remember thinking that if you rolled up a newspaper and stuck it under his arm, he would look like some guy who just woke up, walked to the curb for his paper, and was heading back to the kitchen to read and relax as a part of his slow roll into the day.

He was that kind of laid back and unassuming.

And he *dominated* the tournament.

Royce Gracie, the Brazillian Jiu-Jitsu specialist who was defending the title he'd earned in the first Ultimate Fighting Championship, picked up where he'd left off there and blew through the usually much larger, usually much stronger, usually much tougher looking (and talking) competition.

Needless to say, I was hooked.

Gracie was so good that it seemed almost unfair. His grappling technique was far advanced beyond what the competition – mostly dedicated masters of their respective disciplines, mind you – could handle. He was patient. He was   focused.   And   no   matter   how   the   fights   may   have looked early on, they all ended with his opponents submitting. One after another, he broke them. He made 'em quit.

UNAPOLOGETIC APOLOGETIC JIU-JITSU

. . . Christ, **in whom** *are hidden* **all** **the treasures of wisdom and knowledge***.*

COLOSSIANS 2:2-3
(EMPHASIS ADDED)

The fear of the Lord is **the beginning** *of knowledge…*

PROVERBS 1:7
(EMPHASIS ADDED)

"God is not *the god that we reason* to*; He is the God that we* cannot reason without*."*

SYE TENBRUGGENCATE
(EMPHASIS ADDED)

Sometimes fights are lopsided. Sometimes they are *very* lopsided. Sometimes they are so ridiculously, almost comically one-sided that any observers taking notice of the confrontation, like at a UFC event, for example, can become disinterested, bored, empathetic towards the one being dominated, and even frustrated at some level with the one delivering the whuppin'. They want to see the guy on the short end of the stick show some spark or sign of worthiness to be in the arena in the first place. They feel bad for him. They feel sorry for him. They wish he could do something – *anything* – to at least make the contest even *slightly* competitive; to offer some sort of credible resistance to his opponent. No doubt the one on the losing end of the contest, while not at all disinterested or bored by the fight that they are so completely losing is very much inclined to join with the crowd of disappointed spectators in one critical area: Feeling sorry for the loser, which is, in this case, himself.

We all know this feeling. Somewhere along the way, we have ourselves been or witnessed another being thoroughly humiliated in a manner that exposed our professed competence or knowledge as anything but the "elite level" thing that we might have thought it to be just a moment before the whuppin' began.

Now take that sense of exposed weakness, decimated pride, shame and defeat that we've either experienced or witnessed in others, multiply it by roughly 2.5 gajillion, and then you will have in mind something close to what is rolling through the mind of an unbeliever when confronted with the power of a proper biblical apologetic.

While in previous chapters and in those to follow, we have and will address a number of prevalent myths, techniques, and self-delusions of the unbeliever, here and now we are going to focus on the most universally applied strategy of the unbeliever when they are confronted by an actual biblical defense of the essential *Person* of Christ as the prerequisite for *all* knowledge. That strategy is, in a word, *whining*.

Prolific, purposefully distracting *whining* is the over-arching "grand strategy" for the persistent unbeliever. Until and unless his mind is saved through the Gospel, he *will not* stop clinging to the myth of his autonomy, no matter how thoroughly exposed the sheer illogic and insanity of his worldview is revealed to be under the light of the Word made flesh.

First, this is yet another reason for our proclaiming the Gospel command early and often, before, during, and as a centerpiece of our apologetic. If our first hope where the unbeliever is concerned is that they might be supernaturally saved and raised to life, the Gospel must be our focus.

Secondly, for those who persist in their rebellion against the Person of God and rejection of His Gospel command to repent, we must be fully prepared for the all-out, unrelenting rhetorical contortions, arguments, jokes, shots, and derisions all aimed at one thing: Getting the Christian to let go of the choke-hold that is *killing* the unbeliever.

DO NOT LET GO

...in your hearts **honor Christ the Lord as holy***, always being prepared to make a defense to anyone who asks you for a reason for the hope that is in you...*

1 Peter 3:15
(Emphasis added)

Is the Christ-centered apologetic *literally* killing the unbeliever?

No, of course not.

It's much more devastating and much more painful than that. At least it feels that way to the unbeliever. The Christ-centered apologetic mercilessly obliterates every aspect, claim, and pretension of the unbelieving worldview, without exception and without [*ahem*] *apology*. It completely lays waste to the fictional foundations of unbelief. All of them.

This leaves the unrepentant unbeliever in a most desperate position. As is the case with anyone facing the prospect of drowning or suffocation, they will reach out for and grab onto anything available in order to save themselves. Until and unless the Lord supernaturally saves them, in desperation to preserve the mirage of their autonomy, they will do *anything*.

But with logic, truth, morality, and knowledge itself all abandoned in their rejection of the Person of Christ, the unbeliever has nothing to grab on to. He has nothing to work with. He has nowhere to go.

So long as the Christian maintains his hold through the Christ-centered apologetic, the unbeliever can go nowhere, do nothing, and make not even the beginning of a credible defense for anything in his unbelieving mind.

While we will explain the "signature hold" of the Christ-centered apologetic and its devastating effect on unbelief in future sections, before we go there in detail it is important to hammer home the point that it is essential to never let go of this hold. No matter how loud the unbeliever howls, how much he mocks your persistence, or how much he impugns your integrity, character, intellect or anything else, ***never let go***.

REALLY, DO <u>NOT</u> LET GO

*And Peter answered him, "Lord, if it is you, command me to come to you on the water." He said, "Come." So **Peter got out of the boat and walked on the water** and came to Jesus. **But when he saw the wind, he was afraid**, and beginning to sink he cried out, "Lord, save me." Jesus immediately reached out his hand and took hold of him, saying to him, "O you of little faith, why did you doubt?"*

MATTHEW 14:28-31
(EMPHASIS ADDED)

Early on we focused at length on the primary guiding principle of the Christ-centered apologetic: **We must have an unwavering focus on the *Person* of Jesus Christ.** He is literally, *personally* the answer to the question, "What is truth?" (Which probably then ought to be corrected to, "*Who* is truth?")

The second principle that we're aiming to drumbeat home here is: **We must *never* let go of Him as the *personification*, and therefore *the personal foundation*, of *all* truth and *all* knowledge.**

When we take our eyes, minds, or *apologetics* off of Him for even an instant, we are in serious danger and we are demonstrating our own unbelief. This cannot be emphasized enough.

When the essential nature of the Person of Christ to the very existence of truth, knowledge, or morality is dismissed by the unbeliever, we must not waver. Dismissals of Truth are always inherently incoherent. Any approach that the unbeliever takes to justify the dismissal of Truth will result in spectacular failure...so long the believer holds fast to the Person of Truth in the Christ-centered apologetic.

The unbeliever will squirm, protest, mock, and do everything within his power to convince the believer to let go of the Person of Truth as the foundation of truth so that they can have "a real conversation". We must never agree to this, as to do so is to allow assured victory (all glory to God) to be given away in pursuit of a "real conversation" with someone whose worldview has no foundational basis for reality, conversation, or anything else.

NO REALLY, <u>NEVER EVER EVER LET GO</u>

"A truly Christian defense of the faith must never fail to exalt Christ as Lord over all, including argumentation and reasoning. An apologetic that builds on any other rock than Christ does not honor the greatness of divine wisdom; it is foolishly and audaciously erected on the ruinous sands of human authority."

GREG L. BAHNSEN

The fact of Jesus Christ as the personal source of all knowledge, truth, and wisdom renders all opposing worldviews – and their defense – *impossible*. With no basis for truth and knowledge claims, the unbeliever is in the proverbial wet paper bag, but is unable to even *begin* to punch his way out. This tends to make him a bit cranky.

When an unbeliever is *required* to present their basis for truth or knowledge claims apart from Christ, and they are not allowed to wiggle past or skip over their presentation of the foundation upon which all else must be built, they may well hoot, howl, and protest loudly along the way, but they will be exposed as having embraced a form of insanity (or willful idiocy, also known as *foolishness*) in their pursuit of autonomy. As their egos and pride rail against this unfolding reality, they will lash out and do everything possible to inspire the believer to relax his reliance upon the Person of Christ just a little bit here or on one tiny point of contention over there. We must *never* oblige the unbeliever in this.

In Section Four, we will explore in some detail the nature and effectiveness of the Christ-centered apologetic in demonstrating the impossibility of all wannabe/imagined competitors. Before we get there, however, we will take some time to elaborate upon and examine the dangers and consequences of some man-centered apologetics that have become wildly popular in America and the West over the past several decades.

SECTION 3

THE CASE AGAINST JUDGING GOD

"Nor, again, may we present the faith as a philosophy, to be accepted (if at all) on grounds of rational demonstration; we must always declare it as revealed truth, divinely mysterious and transcending reason's power to verify, to be received humbly on the authority of God. Faith involves the renunciation of intellectual self-sufficiency; we must always proclaim the gospel in a way that makes this clear."

J.I. PACKER

Meology vs. Theology

putting God on trial and man on the throne

"The ancient man approached God (or even the gods) as the accused person approaches his judge. For the modern man the roles are reversed. He is the judge: God is in the dock. . . The trial may even end in God's acquittal. But the important thing is that Man is on the bench and God in the dock."[1]

C.S. LEWIS

---

[1] C.S. Lewis, *God in the Dock: Essays on Theology and Ethics*, ed. W. Hooper, 244

"Presuppositionalism does not require us to consign God to the dock, awaiting the verdict of an autonomous rebel. Instead, it constantly reminds us that sinful man is in the dock before the awesome bar of God's scrutiny and judgment. It encounters him with the intellectual challenge of the gospel."[2]

GREG L. BAHNSEN

All sin is a result of prideful man's pursuit of autonomy. The fallen human heart, in its naturally self-referential state, cannot help but act out in prideful pursuit of the role of god over their own lives. As such, they seek to procure the specific titles and position of God for themselves. One of the titles of God most coveted by would-be autonomous men is that of *Judge*.

I AM vs. I Wish I Was

"*Personally, I* think it's far more logical to draw conclusions based on the evidence. **Let's not believe in the authority of the Bible merely because the Bible claims to be true**. Let's look at modern cosmology, physics, biochemistry, and genetics, all of which point powerfully toward *a* supernatural creator who looks suspiciously like the God of the Bible."

LEE STROBEL, AUTHOR OF *THE CASE FOR CHRIST*
(EMPHASIS ADDED)

---

[2] Greg L. Bahnsen, *Presuppositional Apologetics*, ed. Joel McDurmon, 23

"We're gonna show, through two scientific arguments and one philosophical argument that there's a spaceless, timeless, immaterial, powerful, moral, personal, intelligent creator out there, and **we're not gonna use the Bible to show you that evidence**. We're just gonna give *you* the evidence and let *you* see where it leads."

FRANK TUREK, APOLOGIST
(EMPHASIS ADDED)

"Again it is written, '*You shall not put the Lord your God to the test.*'"

JESUS, IN MATTHEW 4:7
(EMPHASIS ADDED)

The formula of man-centeredness is simple: *I am*.

I am the judge. *I* am the jury. *I* decide what is true for me. *I* decide what is right for me. *I* decide what is moral for me. *I* define and measure all evidence by the standards *I* accept as *I* see fit, because *I am*...

Validation of the man-centered "I am" is impossible to miss in the man-centered apologetics that have come to permeate the popular professing Christian subculture in America and the West.

Whether the man-centeredness of most contemporary apologetics is noticed, understood, or intended by its practitioners (a group which included the author of this book at one time, it should be noted), is not the point. It is very likely that many of those most identified with the man-centered apologetics critiqued here are indeed true believers and lovers of the Lord. The point of focus here is that man-centered, philosophical approaches to apologetics are built upon a foundation that exalts the "I am" of   the   wannabe autonomous rebel above the I AM of Scripture, Who is the *personal* source and standard of all knowledge, truth, and beauty.

It exalts the person of man while diminishing the Person of God. This "if one goes up, then the other must come down" see-saw principle is always the case when it comes to the presentation of fallen man as anything better than what the Bible describes him to be (see: Chapter Two and its discussion of the biblical identifiers of the nature of man, including: "Slave to sin" (Romans 6:17), "Hater of God" (Romans 1:30), "Hater of Christ" (John 15: 18-20), "Hater of Christians" (Matthew 10:22), "Child of Wrath" (Ephesians 2:3) and "Child of the Devil" (1 John 3:10)).

Bad theology produces bad apologetics. Every flaw in theology will produce flaws in apologetics. This is inevitable, as theology – the very nature of the one and only true *personal* God – is, as the Word makes plain, the source of *all* knowledge.

BAD THEOLOGY AND THE SEE-SAW PRINCIPLE

He must increase, but I must decrease.

JOHN 3:30

"Far too often apologists have failed to recognize the unavoidable and reciprocal relation between one's theological system and his apologetic method. The result has been methodological inconsistency: a different epistemology for expounding the faith than that used in defending the faith. However, we must not defend our *message* – that Christ's word is   self-attesting and possessing the ultimate authority of the Lord – with a *method* that works counter to it – by claiming an ultimate epistemological standard outside of Christ's word of truth."[3]

GREG L. BAHNSEN

Dr.. Donald Grey Barnhouse explained the see-saw principle this way:

We have long since adopted the old-fashioned method of the seesaw to test all doctrines. When children are riding two ends of a plank on a seesaw, we know that if one end is down the other is up, and if the first is up the second is down. So it is in the matter of all doctrines. There is an entire set of doctrinal interpretations, which exalts man and abases God, and there is another set that exalts God and abases man. We may be absolutely sure that the path of truth, **in every case**, exalts God. How far did man fall? Only part way, say some, so that he still has the power within his lovable self to lift himself back to God. Man is up in that interpretation, and God is down. **But did man fall all the way, so that not one man could ever have been saved unless God had moved to do it all? That abases man to the place where God has said he is, but it exalts God, and that is the true interpretation of the Word of God. The same rule of interpretation may be applied to all the doctrines in theology.**[4] (Emphasis added.)

---

[3] Greg L. Bahnsen, *Presuppositional Apologetics*, ed. Joel McDurmon, 12

[4] Donald Grey Barnhouse, The Invisible War (Grand Rapids: Zondervan, 1965), p. 119

Fidelity to our Lord and a true love for the lost requires that we embrace and proclaim the truth about man, the truth about God, and, consequently, the complete necessity of the *whole* Gospel, as He has proclaimed these things in His Word.

We do no favors to the Lord who needs none when we try to be "smarter", "better", or "nicer" than the Word in our approach to apologetics. To dismiss the Word is to malign the Word made flesh, Jesus Christ. To claim that He can be improved upon through appeals to those He describes as God-hating, sin-loving, children of the devil is patently absurd and, more importantly, an open insult to the Lord we claim to love. And make no mistake: the watching, sin-loving world notices, and enjoys, such Truth-mocking contradictions.

We must resist the natural, predictable impulse to appease the world by allowing it to sit in judgment over God and His Word.

The apologist Cornelius Van Til expressed concern about a man-centered approach to apologetics through much of his life and academic career, including the following insight:

> "The traditional method…is based on the assumption that man has some measure of autonomy, that the space-time world is in some measure 'contingent' and that man must create for himself his own epistemology in an ultimate sense.
>
> The traditional method was concessive on these basic points on which it should have demanded surrender! As such, it was always self-frustrating. The traditional method had explicitly built into it the right and ability of the natural man, apart from the work of the Spirit of God, to be the judge of the claim of the authoritative Word of God. It is man who, by means of his self-

established intellectual tools, puts his 'stamp of approval' on the Word of God and then, only after that grand act, does he listen to it. God's Word must first pass man's tests of good and evil, truth and falsity. But once you tell a non-Christian this, why should he be worried by anything else that you say? [sic] You have already told him he is quite all right just the way he is! Then Scripture is not correct when it talks of 'darkened minds,' 'willful ignorance,' 'dead men,' and 'blind people'! With this method the correctness of the natural man's problematic is endorsed. That is all he needs to reject the Christian faith."[5]

Thus Saith the Lord!

vs.

Well, Whaddaya Think?

*"**We're not arguing for Christianity**. . .* we are arguing for a generic, monotheism that is affirmed by Jews, Christians, Muslims, deists, theists of every sort."

WILLIAM LANE CRAIG, APOLOGIST
(EMPHASIS ADDED)

---

[5] Cornelius Van Til, "My Credo," *Jerusalem and Athens*, ed. E.R. Geehan, 11

Trust in the Lord with all your heart,
and ***do not lean on your own understanding.***
In all your ways acknowledge him,
and he will make straight your paths.

PROVERBS 3:5-6
(EMPHASIS ADDED)

The Christ-centered apologetic is *not* about arguing for *a god*. It is not about arguing for generic theism, deism, or any other sort of self-exalting, Christ-rejecting worldview or belief. It is not about passing the tests or meeting the intellectual criteria of the debased unbeliever. Generic deists and generic theists (mono- or otherwise) go to hell when they die. Their deism and theism is just as God-hating and Christ-denying, and therefore just as properly damning, as any other form of insanity embraced by unrepentant rebels throughout human history.

The Christ-centered apologetic is about proclaiming the *impossibility* of all of those counterfeits by pointing to the clear, convicting, supernatural *Person and Word of the God that everyone knows*.

The (not so) Great I (probably) Am

the man-centered myth of the "probably god"

> "By appealing to probability, apologists saw Christianity relegated to the museum of mere religious hypotheses (i.e., "possibilities") rather than embraced as the actual truth of God."
>
> GREG L. BAHNSEN

Remember that ridiculously annoying little kid who just wouldn't stop asking *why*? How every answer you gave to him was met with another in a never-ending stream of *why*?

"Why do we eat chickens?"

"Well, we eat chickens because our bodies need food."

"Why?"

"Because God made us that way."

"Why?"

"Because He wants us to be aware of our need for sustenance every day."

"Why?"

"Because our need for food points us to Him."

"Why?"

"Because everything in His creation demonstrates truths about Him and our need for Him."

"Why?"

"Because He wants to show us more and more about Himself as we live our lives."

"Why?"

"Because He knows that we can only grow in joy by growing in knowledge of Him."

"Why?"

"Because God is the personal source of all true beauty and goodness, and He wants us to know that. He wants us to learn more and more about Him so that we can be more and more joyful."

"Why?"

"Because He loves us."

"Why?"

"I have no idea after talking with you for the past five minutes."

Okay, you never said that last part (hopefully), but you probably thought it or something like it.

You may be both interested and horrified to know that the little Perpetual Why Machine with whom you were conversing was actually, by God's grace, teaching you an important epistemological and theological lesson: The lesson of the never ending why, also known as *infinite regression*.

The Infinite Uncertainty of Infinite Regression

"If you don't start with God, your worldview is absurd."

SYE TENBRUGGENCATE

If we are 80% certain of a thing, then we are not truly certain of it. We do **not** know it to be true. It's kind of like being 80% pregnant. 80% certainty is no more a credible claim to true certainty than 80% pregnancy is coherent description of true pregnancy. We may often use the term "certain", but, most of the time, we are not actually referring to true certainty when we do.

Anything we *think* to be true, but are not *absolutely certain* to be true, may, in fact, be false. The same goes for anything of which we are 75% certain, 90% certain, 99% certain, or 99.9999999% certain. The lack of complete certainty allows only for *uncertain* confidence and conclusions, and the only way to have complete certainty of *anything* is to have complete certainty or knowledge of *all* things. In order to have complete certainty, we must know *all* things…or have a flawless, sufficient revelation from One who does.

Our problem as people is that *all* finite beings are limited in knowledge and are therefore precluded from the first option. The best that they can do is give a reason or reasons for their belief in a thing. Then, when pressed to establish the credibility of the first reason for belief in the original thing, they have to give a reason for believing the reason for belief in the original thing. If pressed, logic dictates that this process must go on infinitely, as A would be justified by B, which would then be validated by C, which would then be supported by D, and so on…*forever*…

This is known as *infinite regression*, and it is impossible to avoid for finite beings like you and I when left to our own limited little minds and understanding. Yet we *have* certainty because One who *does* know all things has *personally revealed truth to us*. This will be explored in more detail in future chapters. At this point, however, it is important to note that mere ***probabilities, however compelling or "almost certain" they may seem, never produce or lead to certainty***.

When it comes to the pursuit of certainty or truth, probabilities are *infinitely* frustrating.

We tend to miss the dramatic difference between certainty and probability in part because as people who bear the image of God and live in and as a part of His creation, we ***all*** (believers and unbelievers alike) have been given enough knowledge of Him to justify and embrace a legitimate and true sense of certainty. We are certain of many things because they are certain *in His Person* as reflected in His creation. Even those who deny Him understand this at a fundamental level because He has made them in His likeness. Thus, He is inescapable and undeniable.

Yet when we skip or gloss over Him as the basis for certainty in crafting arguments for anything, particularly a defense of the faith, we have taken an impossible-to-reconcile detour away from the *personal* nature of Truth that is Christ Jesus. In such instances, we have abandoned the one and only source of certainty in pursuit of the mirage that certainty is possible or attainable apart from *beginning* with Christ. In effect, we step off the *personal* Rock foundation of our worldview – Jesus – and onto the wannabe autonomous person's self-referential foundation of shifting quicksand.

We must not allow the professed unbeliever's basis for certainty to go unchallenged. If we love our Lord and love the unbeliever, we must actively, persistently expose that his only basis for certainty is *the God he knows exists*.

The God of Certainty

vs.

The god of Probability

". . . the apologetic task will consist, *not* of *externally verifying* the Christian presupposition but, of *applying* it by (1) bringing God's truth and commands to bear upon the lives of unbelievers, appealing to the image of God in them (distinguishing between present remnants of man's original nature and the ever-present nature of fallen man), pointing out that every fact of the world bears witness to God, and (2) doing an internal critique of the non-Christian's system, calling down its idols, and pointing out the absolute necessity of Christian presuppositions if logic, factuality, history, science, and morality are to have any meaning, validity, and application at all. The Christian apologetic will not concede intellectual ground to Christianity's cultured despisers or allow them to exploit theoretical foundations to which they have no legitimate claim without depending on the Christian faith. Thus, part of the Christian's reasoned defense of the faith will be an aggressive offense."[6]

GREG L. BAHNSEN

The "probably god" of most contemporary apologetics is nowhere proclaimed in the Scripture. The God of the Bible embodies *all* truth. He is the *beginning* of all knowledge and wisdom. He never "makes a case" to plead before the "neutral", "autonomous" man sitting ably on his little

---

[6] Greg L. Bahnsen, *Presuppositional Apologetics*, ed. Joel McDurmon, 6

throne of judgment, ready to capably pronounce judgment upon the Creator.

Embracing the Romans 1 proclamation that "all know God" is to inherently reject the notion of any "probable god" that we might be tempted in our flesh to accommodate.

The perfect Word of the one true God proclaims His perfect, personal Nature, and makes plain that all opposing contentions are sheer foolishness born of the depraved minds of men who, in their sin-enslaved state, will not bend their knee to the God they *know* exists...the God who is revealed throughout His material and immaterial creation as the *necessary prerequisite for all knowledge...*

SECTION 4

CREATION'S REVELATION
The Nature of God on Immaterial Display

"Let this point therefore stand: that those whom the Holy Spirit has inwardly taught truly rest upon Scripture, and that Scripture indeed is self-authenticated; hence, it is not right to subject it to proof and reasoning."

JOHN CALVIN

He Is, Therefore We Think

the nature and necessity of knowledge and logic

"The content and logic of our apologetic comes from the Word of Christ our Lord. This Word of Christ has a unique status among all other words that men may speak, for Christ is metaphysically the Lord (John 1:1-3; Col. 1:16; Rom. 11:36; 1 Cor 8:6), ethically the Lord (Ps. 145:17; Rom. 7:12; Matt 5:17-20; 1 John 5:1-3), and epistemologically the Lord (Col. 2:3; Rom. 11:33; Ps. 147:5; Acts 15:18; Ezekiel 11:5)."[7]

GREG L. BAHNSEN

---

[7] Greg L. Bahnsen, *Presuppositional Apologetics*, ed. Joel McDurmon, 26, 27

e· pis· te· mol· o· gy [ih-pis-*tuh*-**mol**-*uh*-jee]

noun a branch of philosophy that investigates the origin, nature, methods, and limits of human knowledge.

With the literal truth of Jesus Christ *personally* being "the beginning of knowledge", Christian apologetics and epistemology are given form. As Christ is the personal source and revelation of *all* knowledge, we understand that, apart from Him, *nothing* can be known.

This is why He describes those who reject Him as *fools*. This is why He describes them as *blind*. This is why He describes them as *incapable* of right thinking. Until and unless He supernaturally intervenes and raises their dead minds and souls to life, they will remain in a foolish, blind state of inability to submit to Him. Left there, they will never experience the sanity of coherence.

Christ is both Truth and the means by which we know truth.

Regeneration of the dead mind of the spiritually dead unbeliever is the only solution to unbelief. By His grace and for His glory, Christ has ordained the means by which that regeneration of His people will occur: The Gospel.

As we lovingly obey His command to proclaim His Gospel so that His people might be saved from the darkness and insanity of the pursuit of autonomy, we must be prepared to present that ongoing, coherent Gospel proclamation in conjunction with a consistent, biblically coherent apologetic and defense of the faith.

When it comes to epistemological questions, let not your heart be troubled! Do not let the twenty-five-dollar word fool you. The subject of the origin and nature of knowledge is *easy* to address...so long as we rely on the simple, clear revelation that He has given us of Himself.

Every time an unbeliever makes a claim to knowledge – *any* claim to knowledge, they are unknowingly, unwittingly swinging the enemy fortress' gate wide open and *begging* us to invade. And, by the grace of God, *they do this all the time*.

We must graciously accept and eagerly seize the opportunity to pillage an enemy position each and every time such an invitation is extended.

The Unbeliever's Denial of Knowledge
...While Making Knowledge Claims

"Philosophy has been at it for four thousand years and still can't tell you what knowledge is or how you know anything."

K. Scott Oliphint

Answer not a fool according to his folly,
lest you be like him yourself.

Answer a fool according to his folly,
lest he be wise in his own eyes.

Proverbs 26:4-5

We think, pursue knowledge, and make knowledge claims in light of what has been revealed to us through the Person of Christ because we are made in His image. Without Him, we could know *nothing*. Because of Him, we know everything that we know, and we desire to know more. We can only truly have and love knowledge when we truly have and love Him.

One thing we know by His personal revelation is that *fools despise wisdom and instruction.*

Which fools are we talking about here? The ones who deny that the "fear of the Lord is the beginning of knowledge." The context of Proverbs 1:7 is crystal clear. These people despise wisdom because they hate the one and only personal source of all wisdom, the God they know exists: Jesus Christ.

These are also the fools addressed later in Proverbs. In the 26th chapter we are confronted with two critical verses that give us multiple lines of attack in our defense of the faith – a perfect defense that is, truly, an unstoppable offensive. William Edgar addressed the beauty and brilliance of the approach described in verses four and five as follows:

"...First, the apologist must get over onto the ground of the unbeliever for argument's sake and show him that his claims cannot succeed. This does not mean conceding ground, but, rather, patient exploration, as though a particular form of unbelief were true, in order to show how impossible it is...

Second, the apologist should invite the unbeliever over onto Christian ground, for argument's sake, and show him how meaning and value are established by the biblical worldview. This is the equivalent of saying, with the psalmist, 'O taste and see how good the Lord is.' In so many ways, this means preaching the gospel."[8]

Each and every time the unbeliever makes a knowledge claim, we must press him for the basis upon which he can make that claim or any other. Each and every time they make a truth claim or a moral claim, we must do the same.

The fact that an unbeliever thinks is in and of itself an undeniable proclamation of the God he knows exists.

Each and every time an unbeliever makes a knowledge claim, we have the wide-open opportunity and invitation to pillage an enemy position by doing two things:

Answer not a fool according to his folly,
lest you be like him yourself.

PROVERBS 26:4

1. In the spirit of Proverbs 26:4, we are able to point out the folly of his claim to knowledge by demonstrating that he has no **certain** basis for knowledge (see: the infinite regression problem discussed in Chapter Nine), and therefore cannot truly know **anything** at all.

---

[8] William Edgar, Christian Apologetics by Cornelius Van Til, ed. William Edgar, 7

Answer a fool according to his folly,
lest he be wise in his own eyes.

PROVERBS 26:5

2. In the spirit of Proverbs 26:5, having exposed the folly of the unbeliever's claim to knowledge, we can then make plain the impossibility of his worldview by following through its application to any number of everyday realities. This will demonstrate that, among other things, no matter how much the unbeliever may *claim* to embrace his fictional standard of truth and knowledge, he most certainly does not *live* in accord with those principles on a daily, hourly, or even moment by moment basis.

Every truth claim made is an opening. *Every* claim of knowledge or morality is an opening. *Every* claim of *any* kind is an opening.

With these things in mind, let us strive to diligently pillage every enemy position made available to us through the open gate of a claim to knowledge.

All knowledge is of the Lord. Let us never allow any pagan to claim or pretend otherwise.

He Is, Therefore We Judge

the nature and necessity of truth

But who are you, O man, to answer back to God?

ROMANS 9:20

The righteous will rejoice when he sees the vengeance;
he will bathe his feet in the blood of the wicked.
Mankind will say, "Surely there is a reward for the righteous;
surely there is a God who judges on earth."

PSALM 58:10-11
(BOLD EMPHASIS ADDED)

Every judgment made for or against a thing – *anything* – involves making a knowledge claim. Actually, many knowledge claims are required to present even a single judgment in even the simplest form.

As it is God's nature to judge perfectly, and we are reflections of Him, we are imbued with a sense of and desire to pursue righteous judgment. In the believer, this sense and this desire has been fused with the very Person of Christ through His Spirit living within us. He lovingly directs our path and pursuit of truth by His grace and for His glory.

Unbelievers, though claiming an alternative view, understanding, or approach to truth, demonstrate their broken minds' insanity with each and every judgment that they make about *anything*.

Just as all knowledge claims presuppose truth, so too do all judgments, since to make a judgment one must claim to know something about that which is being judged. They must also know something about the standard by which they are making the judgment. So it is that in any proclamation of judgment, the unbeliever must make multiple knowledge claims, and each one of those claims is an open gateway through which the diligent defender of the faith must ride and destroy every enemy position that has been raised against the knowledge of God (2 Corinthians 10:5).

When the unbeliever proclaims *anything* to be good, bad, right, wrong, evil, true, ugly, or false, we must pounce and pillage. We must raze the enemy fortress and conquer the position for the Lord of Glory.

Of course, our pressing of these issues will inspire the hooting and hollering and mocking and evading that we covered earlier, but be must not relent. We must maintain the hold – our hold on the Person of Christ as the basis for all knowledge and all judgment.

Just as the unbeliever radiates his willful idiocy with every claim to knowledge while clinging to a worldview that offers no coherent basis for knowledge claims, he just as flagrantly shouts his own intellectual depravity with every judgment he pronounces against Christ.

12

He Is, Therefore We Learn

~><

the nature and necessity of education and adventure

. . . Christ, in whom are hidden all the treasures of wisdom and knowledge.

COLOSSIANS 2:2-3

*He is the image of the invisible God, the firstborn of all creation. For by him all things were created, in heaven and on earth, **visible and invisible**, whether thrones or dominions or rulers or authorities—all things were created through him and for him. And he is before all things, and in him all things hold together.*

COLOSSIANS 1:15-17
(BOLD EMPHASIS ADDED)

Why do we love all of those books, videos, and presentations of the evidences for God in microbiology, cosmology, history, art, and every other observable, identifiable, *beautiful* realm in His creation?

We love them *because we are Christians*. We have been saved. Our minds have been saved. Our eternal life in Christ *has begun*. Our minds *have been* regenerated, our eyes *have been* opened, and our hearts *have been* inspired to more fully adore the splendor of creation because they have been supernaturally reoriented to adore the splendor of the *Person in Whom*, *by Whom*, and *for Whom* it has *all* been made...every last material and immaterial bit of it.

Believers have been graced with access to *coherent* clarity, joy and hope where the subjects of education, knowledge, adventure, and growth are concerned. Yet even unbelievers, as broken image-bearers of the God they know, cannot help but display His attribute of creativity and cannot help but express their desire to learn more about Him through learning more about His creation, even though they pout about Him all along the way.

Every person's desire for knowledge and pursuit of adventure is born of their being made by Him in His image. Every person's basis for knowledge or purpose for adventure is also rooted in His Nature. Denial of Christ is the denial of the basis for knowledge and the purpose of adventure. These are the truths conveyed in Colossians 22:2-3, Proverbs 1:7, Romans 11:36, and Colossians 1:15-17. The Word here is foundational to all pursuit of knowledge and discovery because Christ, the Word made flesh, is the *personal* basis for all such pursuits.

He is creative, so we are creative. He desires to reveal His nature through His creation of time and all that He has placed *within* it. Therefore we desire to learn, grow, explore, and adore more and more and *more*...there is literally no end or limit to our desire for education and adventure, nor is there any limit to the fulfillment of that desire through Him in the eternal life that we have *now* begun and will continue to enjoy throughout the eternity to come, all by His grace and all for His glory.

That is the future promised His people. *That* is what His people are being groomed for. *That* is the world they anticipate through *Him*. And *that* future is impossible for unbelievers, as it is incompatible with unbelief. The perfect adventure to come will require a perfected cosmos purged of any and all denial of the perfect Light upon Whom it must be centered. So it is that the Lord must and will remove all unbelief and unbelievers before the perfected, eternal adventure will begin for His people in the restored creation over which they will rule.

> ... *for* **the Lord God will be their light, and they will reign forever and ever.**
>
> REVELATION 22:5
(BOLD EMPHASIS ADDED)

Christ is not only the personal basis for the coherent pursuit of education and adventure. He is also the personal source and basis for any coherent desire for extended or eternal life in the first place – a desire shared by all people, believers and unbelievers alike.

As we have seen, the unbeliever's denial of Christ destroys all bases for knowledge. Unbelief destroys the foundation for all knowledge claims. This destruction of knowledge renders the coherent pursuit of education impossible.

The pursuit of autonomy to its end – hell – will leave the unbeliever in an eternal state of bondage – bondage to the supremely hopeless reality of an unending life permanently separated from the pursuit of knowledge, beauty, and adventure that can *only* be known through the *Person* of Christ. Without the possibility of *any* growth through discovery, all hope for a meaningful future is lost. The incomprehensible hopelessness of such an eternity may well be its most defining – and most terrifying – attribute.

The fool who denies Christ denies the basis for truth, knowledge, morality, beauty, and every other good thing in all of creation. Yet in this life, on this side of eternity, the unbeliever is graced by God with the benefits and enjoyment of many of the truths and beauties that they ultimately deny. But when they pass from this life into judgment, their eternity is sealed, and if they make that transition while clinging to the mirage of autonomy, their eternity will be spent in complete separation from even those benefits and beauties that they experience and enjoy now. They will have none of them…eternally. They will know no pleasure. They will know no joy. They will have access to nothing good or beautiful or enjoyable, because they will be eternally separated from the love of the God they know and hate.

This eternal perspective should fuel us. The shockingly stark contrast between the eternity awaiting believers and unbelievers ought to inspire us to passionately, self-sacrificially share the Gospel with each and every Precious Snowflake that we can find…while there is yet time.

> *For the creation waits with eager longing for **the revealing of the sons of God**. For the creation was subjected to futility, not willingly, but because of him who subjected it, in hope that the creation itself will be set free from its bondage to corruption and obtain the freedom of the glory of the children of God. For we know that the whole creation has been groaning together in the pains of childbirth until now. And not only the creation, but **we ourselves, who have the firstfruits of the Spirit, groan inwardly as we wait eagerly for adoption as sons, the redemption of our bodies**.*
>
> ROMANS 8:19-23
> (BOLD EMPHASIS ADDED)

> *But our citizenship is in heaven, and from it we await a Savior, **the Lord Jesus Christ, who <u>will transform our lowly body to be like his glorious body</u>**, by the power that enables him even to subject all things to himself.*
>
> PHILIPPIANS 3:20-21
> (EMPHASIS ADDED)

One day soon we who adore Him will awake *physically* to the realization of these beautiful promises. Yet on the day when *all* are resurrected, believers and unbelievers alike, will we see one more time the faces of men and women and boys and girls with whom we could have but did not share the Gospel? Will our resurrected bodies begin their new life by laying eyes on former "friends" whom we abandoned to the eternal darkness towards which they will on that day be *literally* walking?

SECTION 5

TRUTH RESURRECTED
The Supernatural Life and Gospel of Jesus Christ

"But when the Helper comes, whom I will send to you from the Father, the **Spirit of truth**, who proceeds from the Father, he will bear witness about me. And you also will bear witness, because you have been with me from the beginning."

JESUS, IN JOHN 15:26-27
(BOLD EMPHASIS ADDED)

Supernatural Salvation of the Truth-Hating Mind

the Gospel's restoration of truth, life, beauty and love

"I believe in order to understand."

AUGUSTINE

Before the self-oriented mind can even *begin* to truly think, it must be supernaturally reoriented from the person of self to the Person of Christ as both the basis for its being and the object of its affection. This is only possible through the Gospel.

While our defense of the faith is beautiful and vital because God has ordained it for His glory and our benefit, this defense is not the primary means by which His people will be saved.

We may win arguments, we may "silence fools", and we may bring down enemy strongholds with Christ-centered apologetics. These are all very good things. Yet if we do not purposefully maintain a clear Gospel proclamation of man's evil nature, God's holiness, the coming judgment of a holy God against unrepentant sinners, and the propitiatory sacrifice of God the Son, Jesus Christ, so that His people – those who repent and believe – are saved from that coming judgment, well…we will not add souls to the Kingdom. We may indeed advance the Kingdom in meaningful, eternally significant ways, but we will not add to its eternal population unless we purposefully, practically, and pervasively mingle our apologetic with the Gospel.

Our theology must be biblically rooted and coherent. Our apologetics and Gospel presentations must spring forth from that fidelity to the perfect, consistent, and sufficient "whole counsel of Scripture".

When our theology is grounded in the Person of Christ as revealed in His perfect Word, we will cease to struggle against the truths most offensive to our fallen nature. We will be graciously led by our loving Lord in our life's walk of sanctification. As time passes and maturity grows, we will love many of the truths that we once found most abrasive.

By His grace will learn and love the fact that His glory is more important than anything He has created, including man. We will not measure apologetic success in numbers of debate opponents frustrated or professed conversions attained by persuasion. We will instead measure success by fidelity to God's Word in motive and in action, whatever may come of our presentation where debate details, conversions or concessions are concerned.

Even our Gospel presentation will be liberated from the man-centered measurement of results through numbers and professions of faith.

As we grow in maturity and depth, learning and embracing a Christ-centered apologetic and Christ-centered Gospel as presented in Scripture, we will see more and more clearly with Kingdom eyes. We will think more and more purposefully with Kingdom minds. And we will speak more and more powerfully of Kingdom truth, all by Christ's grace and all for Christ's glory.

Christ-centered; Gospel-fueled

*See to it that no one takes you captive by **philosophy** and empty deceit, **according to human tradition, according to the elemental spirits of the world, and <u>not</u> according to Christ**.*

COLOSSIANS 2:8
(EMPHASIS ADDED)

"You cannot argue for Christianity by giving up Christianity."

SYE TENBRUGGENCATE

The Christ-centered apologetic is a force for the Kingdom's advance on all fronts, because it actively seeks at every opportunity to present the Gospel of Christ through a relentless and unapologetic focus on the Word of God. Through its explicit association with the Person of Christ as its foundation, it always directs the unbeliever to Scripture, where every passage on every subject is ultimately, in context, about the Word made flesh, Jesus Christ.

Man-centered apologetics will encourage men to exalt themselves to the position of judge over God according to their standards. Man-centered apologetics will exalt the mind and philosophies of man as the tools and standards by which God is to be measured and put to the test. Man-centered apologetics will preemptively surrender the Word of God as the authoritative standard by which *all* things must be measured in order to accommodate the madness of autonomy.

The most noteworthy distinction between most man-centered apologetics and the Christ-centered apologetic is, either by its absence or by its presence, open reliance upon the authority of the Word of God.

The Christ-centered apologetic seeks to defend the faith through a faithful proclamation of the authoritative nature of Scripture. The man-centered approach dismisses that authority in an attempt to appeal to the pride and ego of the God-hating rebel.

A Simple Formula for Perfect Success

There is what one might call a "signature move" to Christ-centered apologetics – a move purposely avoided and even openly derided in most man-centered approaches to defending the faith, but a move employed by the Christ-centered apologist again and again, from beginning to the end of any and every apologetic encounter. Apologist Sye TenBruggencate calls it the "two move check-mate". It goes something like this:

1. **Whenever the unbeliever contradicts *anything* in Scripture, respond by saying something like, "That's not what the Bible says."**

2. **When the believer then makes any knowledge claim or judgment in response, ask him, "Where do you get truth without God?"**

And there you have it.

　You want a formula?

　You want a process?

　You want step-by-step?

　There it is.

Straight to Scripture you go. Straight to *truth personified* you go. Straight through the enemy gates swung open with every self-immolating truth claim made by the unbeliever, and straight to the Person of Jesus Christ as the only standard by which *anything* can even *begin* to make sense.

　When *that's* how you're defending the faith, you don't need to worry about "shoe-horning" in the Gospel. Every verse and passage cited will point there, as they are all ultimately about Him, the Word made Flesh.

　Isn't that a beautiful thing?

　Of course it is!

　Beautiful and liberating, to boot!

　No more need to master the subjects of cosmology, microbiology, archeology, or history in order to *hopefully* defend the faith in discussions with unbelieving cosmologists, microbiologists, archeologists, or historians. When we simply believe the Word of God and stand upon it as the authority by which all things are to be judged because Jesus Christ is the *Person* in whom all knowledge is found, we have no need for man-centered games or gimmicks.

The same simple formula will work *every* time it is faithfully used by a true, biblically submissive believer.

We must *believe* the Word.

We must *stand upon* the Word.

We must *defend* the Word.

We must do these things because we adore the *Person* of the Word.

When we do these things on His terms as He provides opportunities, *we will always be successful by* **His** *standards*.

We are all learning. We are all works in progress. Our Lord is infinitely gracious to forgive our sins, including the sins of unbelief we've embraced or enabled in the past, even during our Christian walk of sanctification. This certainly covers past bad apologetic approaches and encounters, so be encouraged. Even *those* things are covered under the "all things" of Romans 8:28, which makes plain that God is sovereign over *everything* and directs it *all* to His ultimate glory and His peoples' ultimate benefit.

When we take our eyes and minds off of Him for even a moment, we are in danger. When we keep our eyes and minds on Him, all good things become possible for us *through* Him.

Let that be our focus – let *Him* be our focus – as we go about the great mission given us to proclaim the Gospel, make disciples, and defend the faith, knowing that He is *personally* with us every step of the way.

And Jesus came and said to them, "**All authority in heaven and on earth has been given to me. Go therefore and make disciples of all nations, baptizing them in the name of the Father and of the Son and of the Holy Spirit, teaching them to observe all that I have commanded you.** *And behold, I am with you always, to the end of the age.*"

MATTHEW 28:18-20
(EMPHASIS ADDED)

ACKNOWLEDGMENTS

I thank God for my beautiful, loving, and most patient wife, Holly, who helped, waited, encouraged, read, critiqued, waited, edited, and waited some more as I spent the hours needed to finish this hopefully helpful little book. She is such an inspiration and blessing to me that I hardly know where to begin to thank the Lord for such a perfect love and helper!

I'm also eternally grateful to our King for my true family, the Church – both the wonderful local body that Holly, Rosie, Wolfgang, and I have been so incredibly blessed to find in Christ the King Church, as well as the more geographically distant Brothers and Sisters who have been such a powerful encouragement and inspiration from afar as this project has come together.

God is so very good both to and through His faithful people. Soli Deo gloria!

ACKNOWLEDGEMENTS

ABOUT THE AUTHOR

Photograph Copyright 2012 Cali Ashton Photography, Nashville, TN

Scott Alan Buss is a wretch saved by grace, a husband to Holly, and father to Rosie and Wolfgang. He and his family make their home in Middle Tennessee, where he is a thankful member of Christ the King Church.

Scott is a writer, speaker, and the founder of R3V Press, where he has published several books. He regularly blogs and podcasts at *Fire Breathing Christian*.

www.FireBreathingChristian.com

FIRE BREATHING

CHRISTIANS

This revised and updated edition of *Fire Breathing Christians* is 416 pages of Christ-centered, Gospel-fueled reformation, revival, and revolution.

ALSO FROM SCOTT ALAN BUSS AND R3VOLUTION PRESS:

There is no "God-given right" to worship false gods. Repent Accordingly.

The America Idol: How "We the People" Made the State Our God in Practice

On Education - Thoughts on Christ as the Essential Core of Children's Education

We Win Here - The Inevitable Triumph of the Gospel in Creation

Candy Christianity - America's Favorite Counterfeit Gospels

The American Child Sacrifice Machine

Fiat Slavery - The Economics of Hell (and America)

Fire Breathing Christians – The Common Believer's Call to Reformation, Revival, and Revolution

Apathetic Christianity: The Zombie Religion of American Churchianity

Satan's Jackass – The Progressive Party's War on Christianity

Stupid Elephant Tricks – The Other Progressive Party's War on Christianity

the

FIRE-BREATHING CHRISTIAN

PODCAST

HELL RAZING RADIO

www.FireBreathingChristian.com

STiCK PEOPLE FOR JESUS
A Tale of Two Churches

See: Matthew 28:18-20; Matthew 6:9-13; 2 Cor 10:5   See: Matthew 7:13-23; Jude 1:4

For more *Stick People for Jesus* comics, visit
www.FireBreathingChristian.com.

Check out the latest Fire Breathing Tees designs
at www.FireBreathingChristian.com

HOME SCHOOL DESIGNS

HOME SCHOOL
A BEAUTIFULLY DANGEROUS THING!

ALL KNOW GOD DESIGNS

ALL
KNOW
GOD

NOT JUST A GOD
BUT THE GOD
ROMANS 1

RAZE HELL DESIGNS

RAZE
HELL

MATT 16:18

BE DANGEROUS DESIGNS

BE DANGEROUS

2 COR 10:3-5

www.ingramcontent.com/pod-product-compliance
Lightning Source LLC
LaVergne TN
LVHW021353080426
835508LV00020B/2272